Grading for
Landscape Architects
and Architects

Grading for Landscape Architects and Architects

Peter Petschek
With a Foreword by Peter Walker

Edited by the
University of Applied
Sciences Rapperswil
Department of Landscape
Architecture

Birkhäuser
Basel · Boston · Berlin

Translation from German into English: Jessica Read, Lindenberg im Allgäu

Library of Congress Control Number: 2008922371

Bibliographic information published by the German National Library
The German National Library lists this publication in the Deutsche Nationalbibliografie; detailed bibliographic data are available on the Internet at http://dnb.d-nb.de.

© 2008 Birkhäuser Verlag AG
Basel · Boston · Berlin
P.O. Box 133, CH-4010 Basel, Schweiz
Part of Springer Science+Business Media

Printed on acid-free paper produced from chlorine-free pulp. TCF ∞

This book is also available in German: „Geländemodellierung für Landschaftsarchitekten und Architekten", ISBN 978-3-7643-8501-9.

Printed in Germany

ISBN: 978-3-7643-8502-6

9 8 7 6 5 4 3 2 1   www.birkhauser.ch

The author would like to
thank the following people
and institutions for their
financial and expert support.

Sponsorship:

Dr. Hermann Mettler, Rector
of the University of Applied
Sciences Rapperswil.

Department of Landscape
Architecture.

ILF Institute for Landscape
and Open Space.

Nik Bokisch, Civil 3D
coordinator Autodesk.

Peter Harradine and Heiko
Heinig from Harradine Golf /
Orient Irrigation Services.

Expertise:

Prof. Sadik Artunc, Clemens
Bornhauser, Prof. Hannes
Böhi, Hans-Peter Burkart,
Michael Fluss, Markus Fries,
Peter Geitz, Heiko Heinig,
Fabienne Kienast, Gabi
Lerch, Rüdiger and Christine
Mach, Thomas Putscher,
Marco Riva, Toni Sacchetti,
Prof. Dr. Hans-Ruedi
Schneider, Prof. Bernd
Schubert, Christian Tack,
Michelle Weber.

Contents

Foreword by Peter Walker

It is with great pleasure that I write this word of introduction to Grading for Landscape Architects and Architects. Certainly the importance of grading to our profession cannot be over estimated.

In my first public project as a young landscape architect in 1960 the grading both set the site plan and produced the human scale of the pedestrian campus. Foothill College in Los Altos Hills, California, near Palo Alto and Stanford University, was one of the first post-war two-year junior colleges, an important aspect of the California educational master plan to expand all higher-education facilities in the state. The site consisted of two rather steep small hills with a series of mature live oak and redwood stands that we intended to preserve. The proposed complex of buildings was too large to fit comfortably on either hilltop and so it was decided to divide the programme, with the academic complex on the northern hill and the athletic cluster to the south; the two were joined by a wooden footbridge. Since there was still not enough level site area, we decided to grade down both hilltops. Our goals were accomplished with a balanced grading plan that aesthetically shaped the site into a beautiful and prize-winning interior campus of rolling lawns and winding paths without the loss of any of the major existing trees.

For thousands of years, earthwork was done by hand. Buildings and roads, farms and fields were generally fitted to the existing contours of the site, which remained largely unmodified. The movement of earth was so expensive that only kings and emperors could afford major projects, such as the famous Imperial gardens outside Beijing.

Then, early in the twentieth century, motorized draglines, bulldozers and trucks began to bring down the price of grading, initially on major public works and strip mines. After World War II, the increased size of the

mechanical equipment further reduced the costs and time required for extensive grading. In the late 1940s earth grading was greatly expanded in the building of roads, complexes of urban and suburban buildings, and in the post-war housing boom. It became cheaper to modify the shape of the land than to fit the building footings to the natural morphology of the site.

Mass grading revised the age-old techniques for dealing with foundation construction, compaction, and drainage and water retention. These new techniques were primarily the domain of engineers and builders. Only a small group of landscape architects and park builders perceived the aesthetic potential for shaping the land. Engineering, mapping and design techniques were generally limited to abstract geometric forms and straight line transitions. "Design" was limited to the balance of cut and fill. Often the "visualization" of the graded form was limited to a series of cross sections depicting only cut and fill. Soil analysis was generally limited to porosity and compaction potentials. Occasionally, organic topsoil was stripped off the graded site (to be replaced later), but usually this was done to remove soil that was difficult or impossible to compact to levels that would support foundations or building slabs.

In contrast, landscape architects from the late eighteenth century on worked with a system of contours displayed on a plan that enabled trained eyes to visualize the shaping of the land, not only to accommodate land uses, but to produce three-dimensional forms of aesthetic importance. Landscape architects made models to visualize the three-dimensional results.

In the 1970s the environmental interest in water use, retention and wetland-aquifer recharging came into public awareness. At first, the is-

Fig. 1.1: Peter Walker during his lecture to the Department of Landscape at the University of Applied Sciences Rapperswil.

sues of erosion and habitat produced a negative reaction to all grading. Then, over the next generation, as scientific knowledge increased in soil science, hydrology, erosion control, planting strategies and rebuilding of habitat, it was possible for landscape architects to design grading and planting strategies of all sizes, from regional scale to specific sites. This has opened up a great new opportunity for shaping an environment conducive to human needs—and also to repair the damage resulting from the crude earth grading and surface mining that characterized much of the work of the twentieth century.

In the post-World War II explosion of development in the United States, earthwork has played a major role in the creation of the modern environment, both for good and for bad. At its worst, millions of trees have been removed, countless millions of cubic metres of topsoil have been lost forever, and in many places drainage and aquifer recharging have been ignored, often resulting in landslides and flooding. At its best, these design techniques have produced elegant parks and recreation areas and reclamation of brownfields and strip mines. The difference between the two outcomes lies in the knowledge, vision and skill of those designing our environment. *Grading for Landscape Architects and Architects* is an important tool for widening knowledge, and thereby the opportunities of site designers, engineers and landscape architects throughout the world.

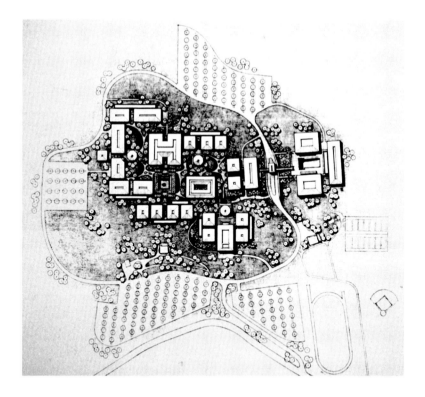

Fig. 1.2: The Foothill College Master Plan was Peter Walkers first public commission and is an excellent example of how grading can inspire design.

Fig. 1.3: The T-Square was an essential piece of drawing equipment for many generations of landscape architects. Peter Walker and the author are shown discussing the development of landscape architecture during his visit to the University of Applied Sciences Rapperswil.

Introduction

Grading plays a key role in landscape architecture. Although the professional spectrum is very broad and grading is not necessarily part of each project, every intervention designed by a landscape architect involves some modification of the earth's surface.

As a basic principle, the interaction of design and ecology with technology and economy lays the foundations for good landscape architecture. This tenet also applies to grading.

Along with vegetation, grading counts as one of the most important design tools with which landscape architects work. Architectural organization principles such as hierarchy, symmetry and asymmetry, or rhythm and repetition can be used in grading. An artificially created hill in the English Garden in Munich appeals powerfully to park visitors. The strolling pedestrian wants to know what can be seen from the top of the hill. The terraces of the Italian Renaissance gardens, defined through levels, embankments and walls, create formal, clearly laid-out spaces, which usually incorporate the views of the surrounding landscapes as an integral part of the design. In contrast, the poetic miniature landscape of the Katsura Rikyu Gardens in Kyoto surprises visitors with ever new views of the lake and buildings on the site. A few steps taken in the garden and the view is suddenly broken by a swell in the ground, only to be replaced by a new scene. Circulation routes are the ideal means of implementing spatial dramaturgy through grading. The English landscape gardeners of the 18th century were masters of manipulating terrain for dramatic circulation. When a path disrupted the view into the distance, it was made to disappear by being sunk out of view. Grazing animals were kept from paths and lawns through ha-has. These trenches, dug with the most basic tools, enabled views without the presence of obtrusive fencing in the landscape, while retaining the cows and sheep as decoration.

Soil is an elementary material in nature's household and the chief building material used in grading. On construction sites, soil is sometimes handled carelessly. This is in part due to the frequent showers and long cold periods of continental Europe, as well as the ubiquitous muck of a construction site. When it is explained in a warm, dry lecture hall that we are dealing with a material of life-giving importance, practitioners willingly give their approval. Weathered rock material mixed with dead and metabolized organic substances, together with air and water, form the product soil. It takes around one thousand years for a few centimeters of topsoil to accumulate. Soil cannot be manufactered and therefore should not be wasted. Nowadays, in most countries building standards and guidelines regulate soil conservation on construction sites.

In addition to light and water, soil is a prerequisite for plant life. The significant role of vegetation in ecological systems should to all intents and purposes be well known to readers. Here are just a few key points:

— Plants produce oxygen
— Plants serve as a food source
— Plants protect the soil
— Plants influence climate

In the context of grading and earthworks it should be pointed out that sensitive grading allows woods, trees and protected vegetation areas to be conserved. As such, grading is an important instrument for ecologically orientated designers.

Fig. 2.1: The Monopterus is a well-known viewing hill and attraction in the English Garden in Munich. Friedrich Ludwig von Sckell, the founder of landscape gardening in Germany, designed the park at the beginning of the 19th century.

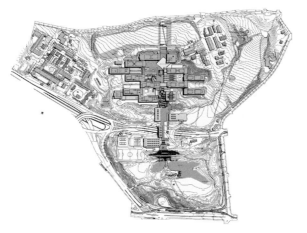

Fig. 2.2 left: Katsura Rikyu was built between 1620 and 1645. It is one of the first accessible gardens of the Edo period and a classic of Japanese garden art.

Fig. 2.3 right: Repetitions in the form of earthworks. Marina Linear Park in San Diego, USA, by Martha Schwartz Partners.

Fig. 2.4 bottom: Earth volume calculations and cut / fill balancing are among the basic technical skills of the landscape architect. In the Irchelpark project in Zurich, designed by asp Landschaftsarchitekten / Neuenschwander, the city insisted that the entire excavation material from the new university buildings be reused on site, for reasons of environmental protection. The material excavated and reused between 1978 and 1985 amounted to 400,000 m³.

"Keep water away from the foundations" is an old and well-known builder's rule of thumb. It only works with well-functioning grading. In antiquity, the Romans constructed roads on earth-filled dams, built up to a meter above the surrounding terrain. The road bed was then laid on top of these dams. Perhaps this is where the word "highway" comes from? Technical competence in surfacing, surface grading, geotechnology, horizontal and vertical road alignment, stormwater management and construction sequence are the basis of good grading in road and pathway construction.

During grading design, economic considerations often cause adverse changes to the local landscape character. In gardens where the client wishes to have a levelled area up to the property line, unattractive prefabricated concrete elements are used to hold back steep slopes.

These ugly retaining walls, which are common in new housing developments, contribute to the interchangeability of places. Roads that cut through hills and mountains to allow for faster travel have small-scale yet accumulative harmful impact on landscape character.

A committed and responsible landscape architecture should pursue meaningful variation, with consideration of design, ecology, technology and economy. Proficiency in grading is an imperative.

"The contour line is the single exact possible representation for the free, natural shaping of a site in plan; so, become proficient with this instrument!" (Loidl 1990, p. 34).

Hans Loidl, landscape architect and professor, formulated this statement in his treatise on landscape design. His declaration is correct, but where and how can I best gain these skills?

In the USA, grading is found in the core curriculum of every accredited university. Students at Bachelor level in European tertiary institutions mostly learn about grading as part of surveying classes. The importance of technical surveying knowledge and site mapping is indisputable. This forms the essential base for all site grading, particularly since the arrival of digital terrain modeling and easy-to-use tacheometers with interfaces to CAD programs. Nevertheless, the strengths of the landscape architect remain in site design. Landscape architects must be in a position to design using contour lines, quickly develop alternatives and evaluate variations based on design, ecology, economy and technology. This can be learnt only through intensive work with contours.

Fig. 2.5 left: A soil section provides information on important soil parameters.

Fig. 2.6 right: Site grading can be learnt only through extensive practice.

History of Site Grading

Developments in Plan Representation

The development of grading plans is closely linked with that of cartography, as the transfer of landform to maps is the most important field of activity for cartographers. In particular, sea maps were of strategic importance in the past and were drawn and updated with the greatest secrecy. In the era of Google Earth™ maps and mobile GPS equipment, it is only with difficulty that we can imagine what life without geoinformation was like.

Initially relief was presented in profile. The famous Swiss cartographer Eduard Imhof (1895–1986) described the typical early mountain symbol as a molehill (Imhof 1965). This landform representation style was adhered to for many centuries. During this period, maps resembled two-dimensional pictures with cities, castles, cloisters, woods and mountains.

An innovation of the Renaissance was the discovery of perspective, which led to a more realistic portrayal of landform. The maps of Tuscany that Leonardo da Vinci drew between 1502 and 1503 are good examples of this new technique. Individual hills and towers typical of the region, and home to the often rival families, are clearly identifiable. These folios are early evidence of perspective in landscape representation.

The transfer of isometric delineation to maps occurred in the 17th century. The military required better mapping to be able to use new weapons technology. Cavalier or military perspective definitively replaced the profile view. The "cavalier" starts with a high parapet of a fortress. From here, the surrounding landscape is visible in half-perspective. Among the best-known illustrations of the age are the town images by Matthäus Merian (1593–1650). The lighting in his etchings always comes diagonally from the left. The resulting play of light and shadow creates a very spatial impression.

By the end of the 18th century, the birds-eye view had superseded the cavalier perspective. The observer's viewpoint shifted upwards.

Since the 19th century, map representation has arrived at plan view. Various hatchings and shading are used to emphasize topography, which

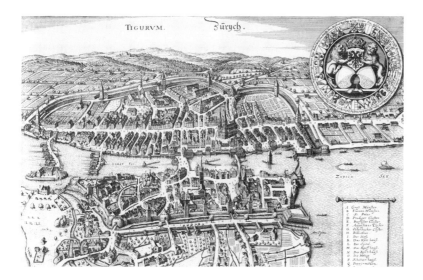

makes reading and understanding the map considerably easier. Slope hatchings are in the direction of the drawn line of the steepest decline. Where there are dramatic relief forms the cartographers use shadow shading. The Dufour map (1844–1864) by the federal chief of staff General Henri Guillaume Dufour, at a scale of 1:100,000 is a fine example of such plastic landform representation. Today, shading is used in combination with contour lines to portray landform on topographical maps. In most maps the lighting is from the northwest so that the relief form is best distinguishable.

Fig. 3.1 left: Konrad Türst's Map of the Federation from 1495/97. This is the oldest map of Switzerland. Even Türst used the molehill technique to represent mountains.

Fig. 3.2 right: Leonardo da Vinci: Codex Madrid. Several folios of Volumes I and II, which were lost until 1965, are land maps of Tuscany.

Fig. 3.3 bottom: A cavalier perspective of Zurich by Matthäus Merian, Topographia Helvetiae, Rhaetiae et Valesiae, 1654.

In parallel to the very effective relief representation techniques, the contour line started to gain importance in the 19th century as a form of elevation information. The determination of spot elevations and the resulting contour lines was made possible by the introduction of an international metric system and an ascertained null datum. Contour lines are lines that connect points of the same height above a reference surface (sea level). Their function is to map the relief of a landscape. The advantage of contour lines is that they deal in quantitative information about the terrain. Other terms for contour lines are isopleth, isoline, isogram, isarithm and isohypse. Lines beneath a zero horizon are known as depth contours or isobaths.

The earliest applicator of contour lines was the Dutch surveyor Nicolaas Cruquius. In 1730 he drew a map of the river Merwede. Using depth soundings, Cruquius measured the depths of the waters and documented his results in the form of contour lines. Today, contour lines are not just to be found in marine charts but are used in a wide range of maps including recreational maps.

Fig. 3.4 left: Dufour map (1844–1864), Matterhorn detail.

Fig. 3.5: The highest point in Switzerland (4634 m above sea level) was named the Dufourspitze in honor of the cartographer General Guillaume-Henri Dufour. The summit is the small, dark rockface in the middle.

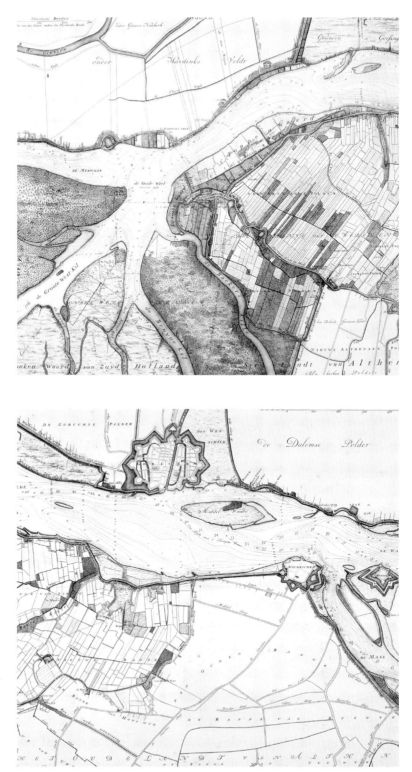

Fig. 3.6 top: The western page of "De Boven-Merwede" by Nicolaas Cruquius, 1730.

Fig. 3.7 bottom: The eastern page of "De Boven-Merwede". These etchings are two of the earliest contour maps.

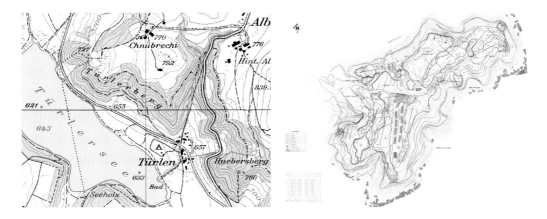

Contour lines are considered to be the cartographical representation of landform. As they communicate a graphical impression of the shape, slope and elevation of the terrain, landscape architects use them to show intended earthworks. With the evolution of computer technology, new working methods and presentation techniques in mapping and planning have been developed.

The first research into digital level mapping was carried out in the late 1950s by C.L. Miller and R.A. Laflamme in the Photogrammetry Laboratory of the Civil Engineering Department of the Massachusetts Institute of Technology M.I.T. (Miller, Laflamme 1958). In the 1960s and 1970s expensive mainframe computers, VAX, McDonnell Douglas und Intergraph computers were needed to compute terrain models. Only universities and large firms were able to afford this technology.

The commercial introduction of personal computers at the beginning of the 1980s gave rise to the IT revolution, and meant that medium-sized and small businesses could acquire computer technology. One of the first PC programs developed for technical drawing was AutoCAD (Version 1.0 – 1982). In the mid 1980s, the mathematician and software writer Kevin Lynch developed the program AutoMap, based on AutoCAD. This program was able to automatically interpolate polylines from x, y, z coordinates and was probably the first PC terrain modeling software.

In 1986, this program caught the interest of David Arnold, David Paine und Terry Bennet of the small engineering consultancy DCA.

Fig. 3.8 left: Coordinate map 1:25,000 (original scale) from the LK25 map sheet 1111 Albis, Swisstopo.

Fig. 3.9 right: Contour line plan (hand drawing) by the golf course designer Peter Harradine.

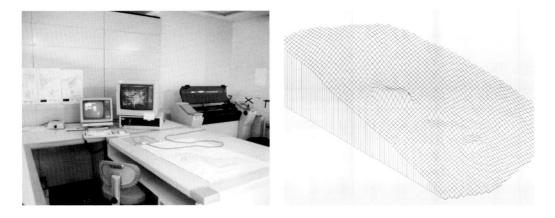

DCA had been formed in 1985. The founders wanted to open up a new niche, with the help of information technology. They started with two IBM PCs, a Calcomp 1098 printer, and two copies of AutoCAD Version 1.5. As the CAD program was not set up for the construction industry, DCA developed survey procedures and a symbol library which they were quickly able to sell to other local firms.

Together with a version of AutoMap released by Lynch, they brought DCA Engineering Software onto the market in 1987. In 1989, DCA Engineering Software purchased the licensing rights to AutoMap, and was known during the 1990s as a software producer in the road and civil engineering industry under the name Softdesk. In 1997 the company was bought out by Autodesk, and together they developed what is now the most popular civil engineering and terrain modeling program in the world, Civil 3D.

Selected Projects

If landform is to be implemented as a design element, it is worth taking a short look back into history. This short selection is in no way exhaustive. The selection criteria were the particular landform and the availability of construction information.

Shaping landform is naturally much older than landscape architecture. Round or oval areas, often terraced into the site, were used in ancient times as performance sites for competitions and theater. However, it was not just the Greeks and Romans who used earthworks to build recreational facilities.

Fig. 3.10 left: CAD workstation in a landscape architecture office in 1988 with a PC (16 MHz, 8 MB RAM, MS-DOS operating system, AutoCAD Version 9), digitizer tablet and pen plotter.

Fig. 3.11 right: DCA site model by the author for a golf course, 1991.

The Pueblo Grande Ball Court

The Hohokam were Native American Indians who cultivated corn, bean, tobacco and cotton in Arizona and northern Mexico up to the 16th century. Pueblo Grande is an archeological excavation of this culture, which lies on the outskirts of what is today Phoenix, Arizona, USA. Together with the affiliated museum, the archeological park documents the life of this now extinct tribe.

From the perspective of grading, the "football pitch" in Pueblo Grande is very interesting. According to museum documentation there are several of these spaces in each Hohokam settlement. Grounds for ball games are found in other excavation sites in Central and North America; however, in these other cases landform is of no importance. The Hohokam "arena" is a long oval (25 to 35 meters), about 15 meters wide and slightly sunk into the ground. The excavated spoils are banked into earth walls up to 3 meters high that surround the arena. As in modern sports arenas, these served as seating for spectators. The large Hohokam arena just outside of Phoenix has earth walls with a spectator capacity of around 500 people. The playing surface of the arena is made smooth through a lime stabilizer and formed like a tub. At both ends of the grounds, small openings formed goals. Similar to soccer, the players tried to get the ball into the opponents' goal. Stone markers in the ground in front of the goals and in the middle of the pitch indicate the play areas. Unfortunately, nothing more remains of the game, as the Hohokam Indians no longer played it when the Spanish conquerors arrived in Arizona in the mid-16th century (Andrews, Bostwick 2000, p. 26). Whoever happens to land at Phoenix airport and is interested in landform should certainly visit the nearby Pueblo Grande!

Fig. 3.12: Adobe settlement in the southwest USA.

Fig. 3.13 top: Hohokam Indian earth arena for ball games in Arizona.

Fig. 3.14 center: The stone in the middle is a play area marker; in the background is a goal.

Fig. 3.15 bottom: The surface is drawn up the sides like a tub and is smooth.

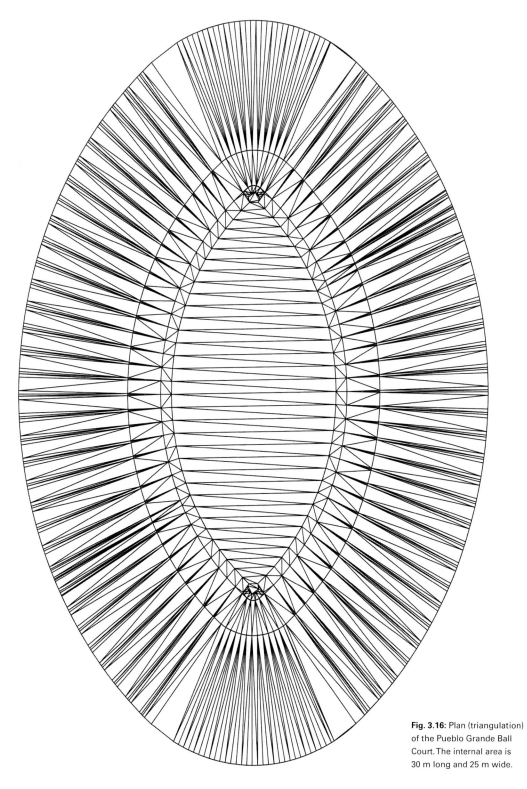

Fig. 3.16: Plan (triangulation) of the Pueblo Grande Ball Court. The internal area is 30 m long and 25 m wide.

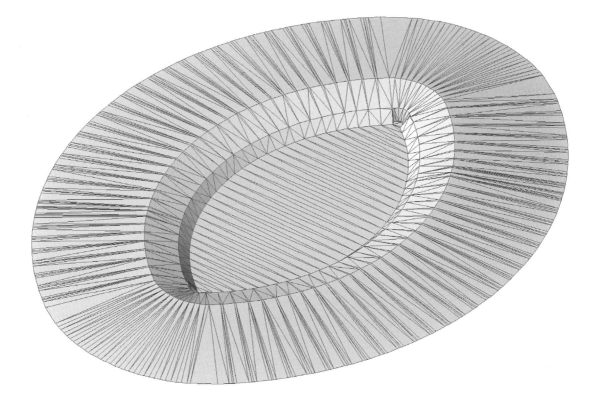

Fig. 3.17: Isometric view of
the shaded triangulation.

The Pyramids of the Branitz Landscape Park

Hermann Fürst von Pückler-Muskau (1785–1871) was a landscape gardener, well-traveled writer, eccentric bon vivant and gourmet. "Very regularly the 24 hours of my day are divided into four parts: one quarter is devoted to parks, another to writing and reading, and the remaining two to sleeping and eating." (Lauer 1996, p. 28). A great enthusiast for the English landscape garden, Pückler-Muskau built two significant parks in Germany in the 19th century. His main work was the garden at the family seat in Muskau. In the book *Andeutungen über Landschaftsgärtnerei* (Suggestions on Landscape Gardening) he expounds on his design principles. Because his expensive lifestyle landed him deep in debt, and despite his tirelessness in perfecting the garden, Pückler eventually had to relinquish the residence in Muskau.

In 1845 he moved to an estate he had inherited in Branitz near Cottbus, around 12 kilometers from Muskau. There, constantly plagued by money troubles, he built his second great garden masterpiece. From 1846 until his death he designed the landscape park in various phases. Landform played a dominant role in this garden.

The Branitz Park features two earthen pyramids: a lake and a land pyramid. The lake pyramid, built between 1856 and 1857, was to serve as his own sepulcher. "So the path to the tumulus is opened to me" were Pückler's last words (Lauer 1996, p. 9). The land pyramid was intended for his wife and was completed in 1863. On the tops of the pyramids Pückler had inscribed: "Tombs are the summits of a distant new world".

Pückler's pyramids relate in function and proportion to the ancient Egyptian burial tombs. The pyramids in Giza were perhaps the archetype

Fig. 3.18 left: The steps up the land pyramid.

Fig. 3.19 right: View from the land pyramid to the lake pyramid.

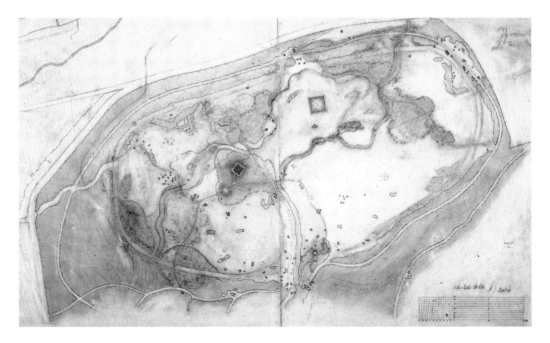

Fig. 3.20: Original pencil drawing from 1866/1867 of Branitz Park with both pyramids shown.

for the water pyramid. These could be reached by boat if the Nile was running high. For the land pyramid, Pückler borrowed from the Egyptian pyramid at Meidum, which protrudes from a mountain of rubble (Tietze 1999, p. 36).

He himself had climbed to the top of the Great Pyramid of Cheops during his trip to the Orient. "But so as to endow here a rarity, which is hardly to be found in the rest of Europe, I arrived at the idea of erecting an ancient tumulus as my tomb, a four-sided pyramid made of earth." (Lauer 1996, p. 9).

Pückler spent 1854 occupying himself with the design of the pyramids. "There is not too much to say about this. The most important thing may be that one must spare them as much as possible. The natural unevennesses of the site are generally more picturesque than that which Art can achieve with much effort. Artificial hills normally have but little effect. However, they may be necessary to obtain a view from the top, to give planting more height or to dispose of the earth spoils from a dug lake." (Pückler-Muskau 1988, p. 137).

The steepness of the lake pyramid led to discussion with his head gardener. Pückler wanted an embankment of 45° (1:1). In the end, the works contract fixed a height of 12.80 meters and a base width of 32 meters, resulting in a slope of 39° (1:1.25). For comparison: in road construction

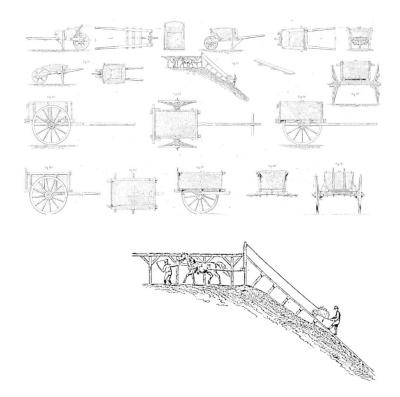

today embankments with a slope of 33.7° (1:1.5) are typical. In addition, the contract contained information about the technical construction of the pyramid: "Soil compaction should be performed with a piling hammer every four feet, and sandy soil should be laid only in the interior of the pyramid. The exterior should be clad with a 3-foot-strong layer of heavy earth." (Neumann 1999, p. 10). Six months were planned for constructing the pyramid. For reasons of economy, the earthworks were accomplished with the help of inmates from the Cottbus penitentiary, using wheelbarrows. "For the laborious earthworks in the park, as a rule about 50 to 60 prisoners were used, and at times up to 120." (Schäfer 1999, p. 137).

Being a landscape gardener and gourmet, physical wellbeing was not to be skimped on: "I spend several hours daily at the pyramid with a jug of beer beside me, as we have very thirsty weather ... you know how much I love that." (Kohlschmidt 1999, p. 194).

The Branitz pyramids are just one example of the numerous earthwork projects of the time. A description of site grading in English landscape parks alone would fill volumes. Nevertheless, Pückler's eccentric earthworks remain one of a kind. In an age without bulldozers and diggers, to have built burial pyramids for oneself and one's wife while at the same time accumulating a mountain of debt is a most unusual bee to have in one's bonnet.

Fig. 3.21 top: In all likelihood, the inmates of the Cottbus penitentiary used "pushcarts" like these to build the pyramids (Henz 1856, plate IV).

Fig. 3.22 bottom: On very steep sites horse power assisted the pushcarts (Henz 1856, plate IV detail).

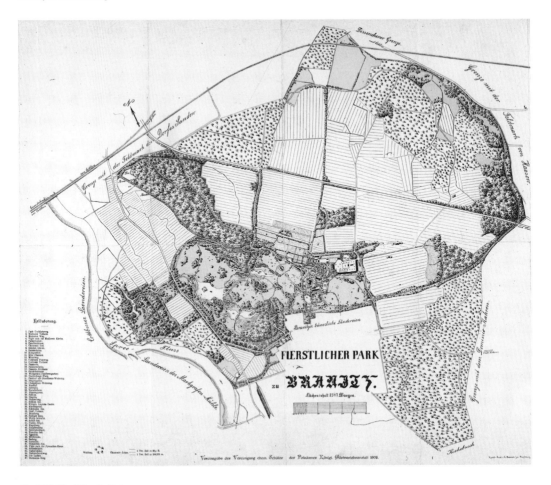

Fig. 3.23: The Princely Park, Branitz Park Plan from 1903, a donation by the Vereinigung ehemaliger Schüler der Potsdamer Königlichen Gärtneranstalt (Association of Former Students of the Potsdam Royal Gardening School).

Fig. 3.24 right top: The tumulus, tableau of the stately home Branitz and its surroundings, 1857. Steel engraving by Poppel and Kurz after a drawing by Gottheil.

Fig. 3.25 right bottom: Tableau of the stately home Branitz and its surroundings, 1863. Steel engraving by Poppel and Kurz after a drawing by Gottheil.

Der Tumulus.

Der Rosenberg.　Der Kiosk.　Das Schloß von der Parkseite.　Das Schwanenhäuschen.　Die Treppensichten.

Die Parkanlagen in Branitz.

Fig. 3.26 top: The lake pyramid in the foreground, the land pyramid in the distance.

Fig. 3.27 center: View of the lake pyramid from the park.

Fig. 3.28 bottom: "Tombs are the summits of a distant new world", reads the engraving on the railing of the land pyramid.

The "Poet's Garden" at the G 59 in Zurich

Two thirds of Switzerland is covered by mountains. On a clear day, the Alpine panorama is breathtaking. Grading is a particular challenge in Switzerland as there are usually huge natural examples right in front of one's nose – except when it is foggy. Ernst Cramer (1898–1985), one of the most important Swiss landscape architects in the 20th century, was asked to design a "Poet's Garden" for the first Swiss Garden Expo G 59. It was not an easy undertaking to create a contemplative space in the middle of a colorful sea of flowers; indeed, the G 59 was tellingly entitled "Flowerland".

The temporary exposition was located on the right shore of Lake Zurich, what is today known as the Blatterwiese. The 2500 m² installation was composed of four grass pyramids, a grass cone, and a flat water basin in which the earth shapes were reflected. The pyramids were 2, 2.8, 3 and 4 meters high. The asymmetrically stepped cone was 3 meters high and 11 meters in diameter. Interestingly, many visitors estimated the pyramids to be twice as high. The perspective effect of the sloped sides certainly contributed to this impression (see Weilacher 2001, p. 108).

"The garden was not so much a garden as sculpture to walk through abstract earth shapes independent of place, with sharp rises foreign to the nature of their material" (Kassler 1964, p. 56). Next to work from Burle Marx and other high-profile landscape architects, architects and artists, the project, with the abstract grass pyramids reflecting in the water surface, was included in a 1964 publication by the Museum of Modern Art, New York titled *Modern Gardens and the Landscape*, and as such achieved world renown.

Fig. 3.29: The grass pyramids in the "Poet's Garden" were very popular with children. Many adult visitors did not understand the abstract garden space.

As no construction documents exist in his estate and according to Fritz Dové, a landscape architect and for many years Cramer's employee, no construction documents were drawn, technical construction details can only be deduced from photographs. Fritz Dové wrote: "The published drawings probably also served as construction drawings. By entering the height of the tops of the pyramids they were useable for the rough grading work, and the final form was influenced by the quantity of available material and the sinking of the fill area", (Fritz Dové, email of August 9, 2007). Furthermore, Dové explains that in any case, Ernst Cramer felt more at home on site than at the drawing table and often made important design decisions in situ. The garden was built by Cramer's own landscape construction firm.

Children frolicking on the earth shapes quickly caused erosion and loss of the precise geometry (see Weilacher 2001, p. 115). To avoid tread damage and to ensure the development of a stable sod, the grass should not have been accessible during the first season. But because it was a temporary garden and had to be built in the shortest possible time, obviously this could not be put into practise.

Despite these structural shortcomings, it should be stated that in his projects Cramer put much emphasis on professional site earthworks. In an interview between the landscape architect Stefan Rotzler and H. J. Barth, a landscape architect who worked for Cramer for five years, Barth made

Fig. 3.30: The "Poet's Garden" shortly before completion.

the following remark: "Plants and earth levels were not some dull task as in other offices, but rather there was a special doctrine of harmonics. For example, an embankment had to become increasingly flat towards the bottom, to produce a very flat embankment base, and the top edge was quite strongly emphasized. This was a very specific motif which E. Cramer paid meticulous attention to" (audiotape transcription, anthos 2/87, p. 5). Unfortunately, in the fall at 1959 at the end of the Garden Expo, Ernst Cramer's trailblazing earthworks were completeley levelled.

Fig. 3.31 top: Sides up to 45° steep made the work on the earth pyramids difficult.

Fig. 3.32 center: The slope top edges were not further stabilized.

Fig. 3.33 bottom: Cramer placed great value on precise site modeling in his construction company.

GARTEN DES POETEN

E. CRAMER GARTENARCHITEKT BSG SWB ZÜRICH

Fig. 3.34 top: Design drawing of the "Poet's Garden" by Ernst Cramer, Zurich.

Fig. 3.35 bottom: Reflection of the earthworks in the garden's water basin.

The Olympiapark in Munich

In addition to defining aesthetics and orientating site use, site grading can also convey a political idea. The Olympiapark in Munich is a good example of this. "The goal of the 1972 Olympiapark in Munich is a contrast in spirit and architecture to the Olympic facilities built for the 1936 Games during Hitler's era. The new facilities were to represent a different Germany, a tolerant, liberal country." (Grzimek 1973, p. 14). The motto of the first big international sporting event in post-war West Germany was "the Happy Games", and ten days long the playfully shaped parking areas typified this idea. Regrettably, a subsequent terrorist attack overshadowed the event.

The Oberwiesenfeld site, situated to the north of Munich's inner city, equals the inner city in area with its 280 hectares (2.5 x 1.5 kilometers). It had been used earlier as a parade ground and sports airfield, and during the Second World War was used as a dump for rubble from destroyed buildings. Apart from a single 60 meters high mountain of debris, the area was flat and bare. The construction of the sports facilities required a lot of excavation, so the flat site lent itself ideally to a new grading concept.

The design and construction of the Olympiapark lasted from May 1968 to August 1972, and while the architects Behnisch & Partner were responsible for the overall master plan, responsibility for the design, construction documentation and construction supervision of the landscape lay with Günther Grzimek (1915–1996). Frei Otto developed the roof construction. The interweaving of landscape and architecture is characteristic: some-

Fig. 3.36: The park's viewing hill made from rubble from the Second World War and the excavation spoil from the Olympic facilities shaped the site.

Fig. 3.37: The tent architecture was designed by the architects and engineers Behnisch & Partner, Frei Otto, Leonardt + Andrä; landscape architecture: Günther Grzimek.

times the landscape seems to flow over the architecture, and at other times the landscape is totally penetrated by the architecture.

Günther Grzimek has explained the "Olympic park idea" in various publications. Amongst other things, he emphasizes the aesthetic of naturalness:

The park is a "place for daily use. Hill and lake, tree and grove, meadow and bog, shore and path, stone and gravel are the building blocks for a landscape that is natural and at the same time hard-wearing, as a good utility object should be." (Grzimek 1984, p. 71). He aspired to create a "user park" and a "utility landscape"; the park was to follow the steps of the people and not the other way round. The park was to instigate spontaneous use, acquisitive use of the lawns was expressly desired. A differentiated path system with main and secondary routes was developed to meet the requirements of both large-scale events and everyday leisure.

A second important point was the revitalization of a metaphor of educational freedom, which also defined the English landscape garden. Symmetry, hierarchy and stone monumentality were avoided. Above all, as much as possible nothing was to be forbidden: "The park allows its users largely free decision-making about their behavior." (Grzimek 1984, p. 70).

Landform design is the main theme of the park. It is this that creates the connection between landscape and architecture, as a few quotes from Grzimek, who also taught as Professor of Landscape Architecture at the Munich University of Technology confirm:

"The relief energy results from the relationship and composition of horizontal and vertical leading lines in the landscape. It increases with the diversity of the surface modeling, the richness of topographical elements, as there are flats, peaks, slopes and depressions, and so on." (Grzimek 1972, p. 11).

"The key concept developed for the Oberwiesenfeld was a continuous dialectic opposition and coexistence of significant topographic elements, whose formal polarity correlates with the contents of 'privacy' and 'communication'." (Grzimek 1972, p. 12).

"Apart from the elementary and inexpensive materials (gravel, stone, grass, trees, bushes), the program was an integral factor in the low construction costs. Large areas of the hill landscapes – the steep mountainsides – were created as wildflower meadows on poor soils. The ground was worked solely with machines. The gravelly soil proved itself highly robust for this purpose." (Grzimek 1984, p. 70).

"A person does not walk rigorously in a straight line, they wander – even without noticing it. They gladly oscillate in the third dimension – but with only 1 to 3° deviance from the flat. When they go up a mountain, then either in a cut – or a long-drawn out hill. One can anticipate the pathways. Nothing is by chance." (Grzimek 1993, p. 32).

"On the grass, people walk differently than when on a designed path. There are no leading lines, so they move according to their feelings and the contours – when this is offered to them." (Grzimek 1993, p. 33).

Fig. 3.38 left: Landform detail of the "utility landscape".

Fig. 3.39 right: The "taking" of the hill during the opening of the Olympiapark.

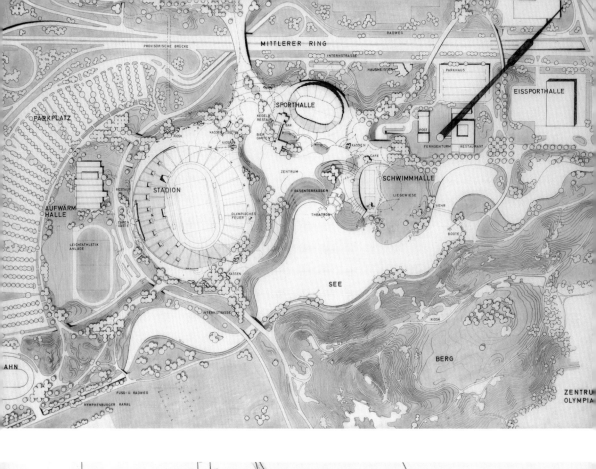

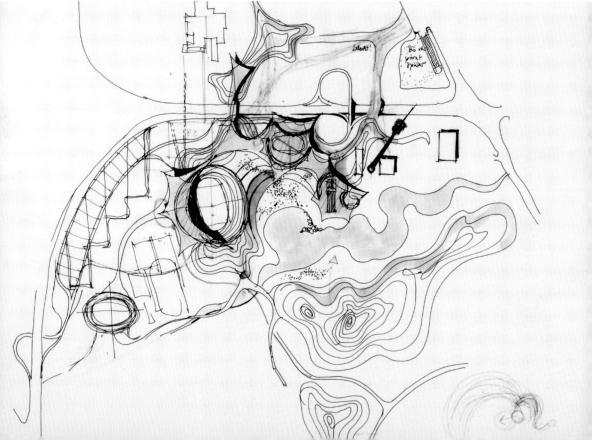

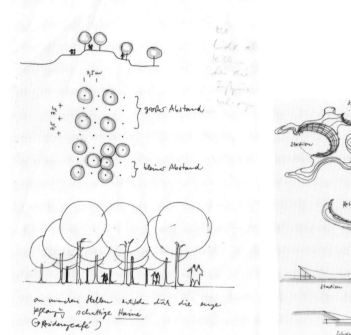

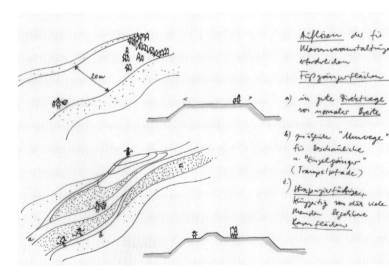

Fig. 3.40 top left: Master plan of the Olympics site Behnisch & Partner, Stuttgart.

Fig. 3.41 bottom left: Concept sketch at 1:2000 by Behnisch & Partner, Stuttgart. Sketch by Carlo Weber.

Fig. 3.42 top middle: different spaces are created using tree spacing and landform. Sketch by Carlo Weber.

Fig. 3.43 top right: The athletic stadiums were envisaged as earthworks with integrated spectator bleaches. Sketch by Carlo Weber.

Fig. 3.44 below: The park has a diverse, use-orientated circulation system ranging from informal trails to pedestrian lanes for large events. Sketch by Carlo Weber.

Fig. 3.45 top: View of the construction site from the lookout hill.

Fig. 3.46 center: The view from the TV tower of the construction site from the upper end of the lake.

Fig. 3.47 bottom: Landscape grading in progress in the fore and middle ground, completed landform creation in the background.

Landform at the Scottish National Gallery of Art in Edinburgh

Charles Jencks is an architectural theorist and is deemed to be the father of postmodern architecture. Over the past few years Jencks has also busied himself practically with landscape architecture. He combines two principles in his artistically shaped landscapes. The first originates from Chinese garden art and is the principle of "borrowed landscape", meaning gardens as miniaturized landscapes. This principle is linked to the characteristic hill and lake landscapes of Scotland. The second principle is that of the wave. For Jencks, the wave is the basic pattern of all life and a metaphor for the entire universe. In an interview Jencks called his work "contour gardening", referring to the hard edges of his graded earth embankments which, particularly at dusk, distinctively trace the shape of the landform (Jencks 2005).

A very impressive landform project designed by Jencks is found in front of the National Gallery for Art in Edinburgh. The Scottish landscape architecture office Ian White Associates was responsible for the project management and construction supervision of the £350,000 project. The planning and construction each lasted one year; the project was completed in 2002. John Farquhar, the project landscape architect from Ian White Associates, wrote:

"As the completed landform was to be accessible to the public, safety and durability issues were critical to the construction process. A detailed site analysis was carried out followed by a rigorous construction methodology to determine the best approach to the works on site. A set of detailed drawings and specifications were prepared for tendering the project to an approved list of civil contractors. The Landform covers approximately 3000 m² (0.75 acres) consisting of 3500 m³ of fill material, stands 7 meters at its

Fig. 3.48: The Scottish National Gallery with the Landform at its entrance is located near the Mound on the edge of the city center of Edinburgh.

highest point and has three shallow serpentine pools holding 1,500,000 liters of water. A recirculation system linking all the pools provides a constant flow of clean water. The integrated irrigation system ensures the greening of the turf.

The generous depth of topsoil across the front of the Gallery site was removed and stored for reuse as rootzone material. The lack of suitable site material to form the mounds necessitated the importing of inert oil shale as fill material. The material is an industrial waste product from the oilshale industry found locally to the west of Edinburgh. It has a very dense composition, is generally 15 millimeters diameter to dust in size, but due to its oily nature provided a cohesive quality for construction. The shale was placed and compacted in 300 millimeters deep layers to the designed profiles.

A series of cross-sections were produced to highlight the varying gradients across the Landform and a local grid was established to provide accurate setting out points for the serpentine ponds. The artist stipulated the steepness of the maximum 45° gradients on the landform. The benching of the layers was neatly finished along edges by hand trimming to form a key for the rootzone material.

The approved profiles were then covered with a 200 millimeters deep layer of manufactured rootzone material comprising site topsoil (4 parts by volume); coarse sand (2 parts by volume) and 7-4 millimeter grit (one half part by volume) accurately batched under cover off site. To this mixture was added polypropylene mesh elements supplied by Netlon Ltd. at a rate of 3.50 kg/m³ to provide the necessary reinforcement to the rooting medium. The material was placed in one layer and accurately trimmed to design grades with a machine, however, care was required to avoid raking out the mesh elements. The finished landform was then inspected and approved prior to the turfing operation.

Fig. 3.49: Landform detail.

The selected turf consisted predominantly of drought resistant cultivars of fescues. Large rolls of turf were positioned on the top ridge and rolled out vertically down the face of the landform and pegged to secure at 600 millimeter centers with 150 millimeters long biodegradable pegs. The joints were filled with a sand-soil mixture.

Public access to the Landform is limited to the opening hours of the Gallery, however, due to health and safety demands access is not permitted when the steep slopes are slippery and wet.

The steepness of the turfed slopes necessitates the use of Flymo lawn mowing machinery on a rope and operated from the top ridge. An integrated irrigation system along the ridge of the landform ensures the greening of the turf. As an installation it does not have a predicted life, but there are renewable items such as pond liners and pumps that will have to be replaced in the future." (John Farquhar, Ian White Associates, email, September 4, 2007).

Fig. 3.50: Landform detail.

Fig. 3.51 bottom: Access to the Landform is normally allowed, not just for swans.

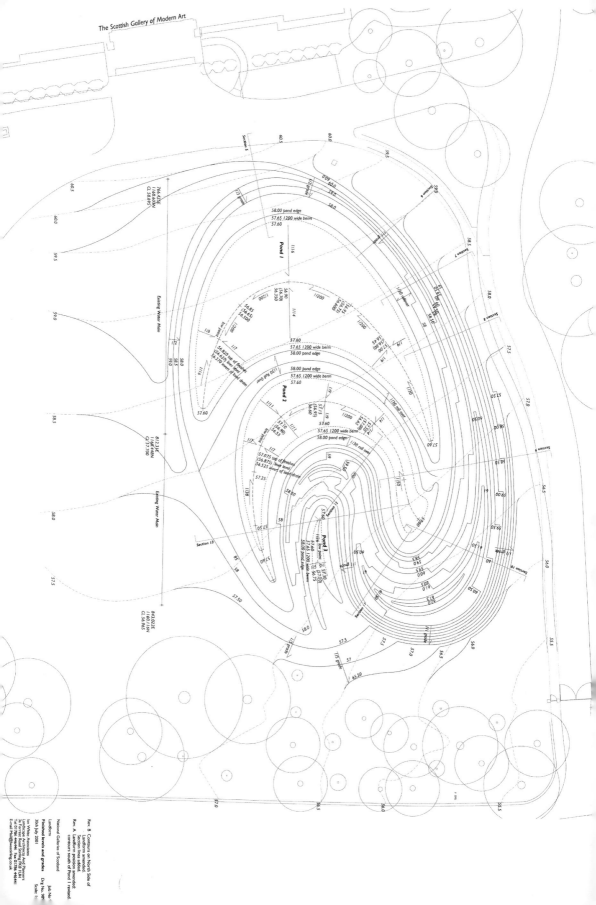

The Scottish Gallery of Modern Art

Pond 1

Pond 2

Pond 3

58.00 pond edge
57.65 1200 wide berm
57.60

57.60 1200 wide berm
58.00 pond edge

58.00 pond edge
57.65 1200 wide berm
57.60

57.60
57.65 1200 wide berm
58.00 pond edge

58.00 pond edge
57.65 1200 wide berm
57.60

57.60
57.65 1200 wide berm
58.00 pond edge

Existing Water Main

Existing Water Main

National Galleries of Scotland

Landform

Finished levels and grades

30th July 2001

Ian White Associates
Landscape Architects And Planners
34 Forrest Road, Stirling FK8 1UH
Tel 01786 446446. Fax 01786 446441
E-mail Mail@iwassoc.demon.co.uk

Rev. B Contours on North Side of
Landform amended.
Section lines added.

Rev. A Landform position amended;
contours south of Pond 1 revised.

Job No: 98
Dwg No: 98
Scale: 1:

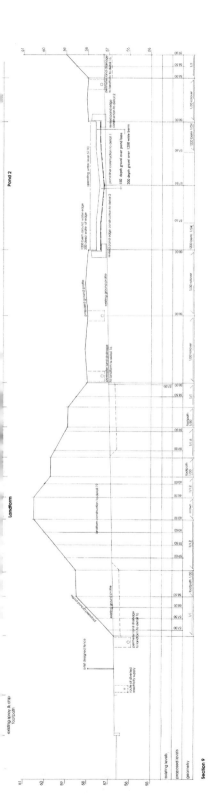

Section 9

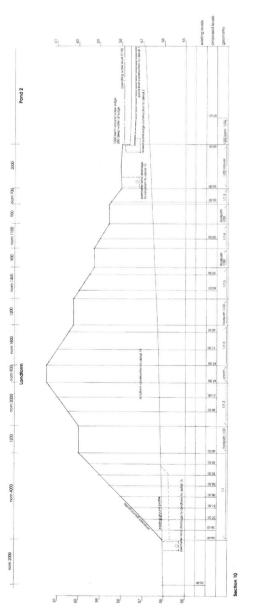

Rev A (RW04/01) AS-BUILT
150/200 depth gravel finishes over liner,subsoil layer deleted

National Galleries of Scotland

Landform

Sections 1/50 (sections 9/10)

July 2001-07-24

Ian White Associates
Landscape Architects & Planners
3A Forest Road, Stirling, FK8 1UH
Tel 01786 446446 Fax 01786 446441

Job no 1989
Dwg no 1989/13
Scale 1/50

Pond 2

Section 10

Pond 2

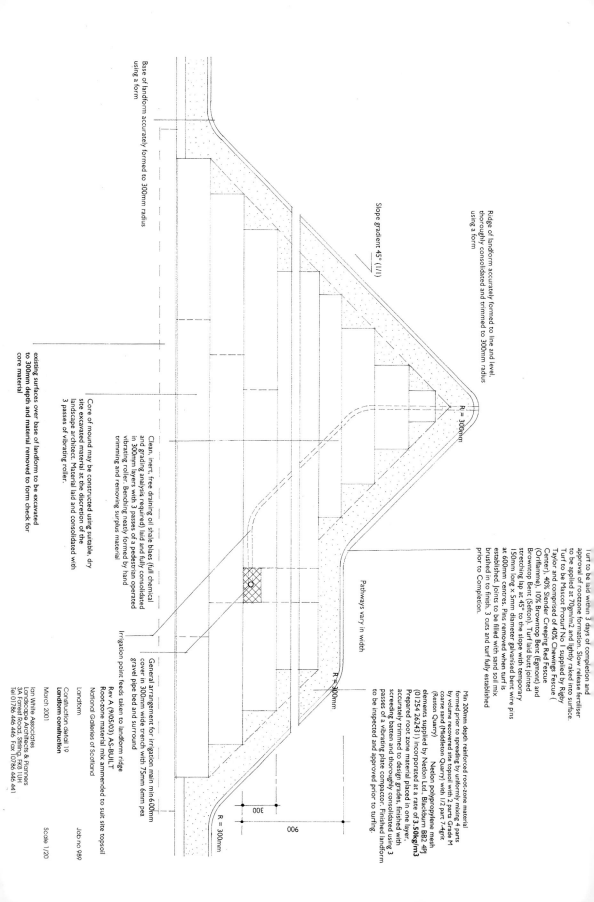

Base of landform accurately formed to 300mm radius using a form

Ridge of landform accurately formed to line and level, thoroughly consolidated and trimmed to 300mm radius using a form

Slope gradient 45° (1/1)

existing surfaces over base of landform to be excavated to 300mm depth and material removed to form check for core material

Core of mound may be constructed using suitable, dry site excavated material at the discretion of the landscape architect. Material laid and consolidated with 3 passes of vibrating roller.

Clean, inert, free draining oil shale blaes (full chemical and grading analysis required) laid and fully consolidated in 300mm layers with 3 passes of a pedestrian operated vibrating roller. Benching, neatly formed by hand trimming and removing surplus material

Pathways vary in width

Irrigation point feeds taken to landform ridge

General arrangement for irrigation main min 600mm cover in 300mm wide trench with 75mm 6mm pea gravel pipe bed and surround

R = 300mm

300

900

Turf to be laid within 3 days of completion and approval of rootzone formation. Slow release fertiliser to be applied at 70gm/m2 and lightly raked into surface. Turf to be Mascot Procurf No I supplied by Rigby Taylor and comprised of 40% Chewings Fescue (Center), 40% Slender Creeping Red Fescue (Oriflamme), 10% Browntop Bent (Egmont) and Browntop Bent (Sefton). Turf laid butt jointed stretching lap at 45° to the slope with temporary 150mm long x 5mm diameter galvanised bent wire pins at 600mm centres. Pins removed when turf is established. Joints to be filled with sand soil mix brushed in to finish. 3 cuts and turf fully established prior to Completion.

Min 200mm depth reinforced root-zone material formed prior to spreading by uniformly mixing 4 parts by volume recovered site topsoil with 2 parts Grade M coarse sand (Middleton Quarry) with 1/2 part 7-4grit (Reston Quarry). Netlon polypropylene mesh elements supplied by Netlon Ltd. Blackburn BB2 4PJ (01254 262431) incorporated at a rate of 3.50kg/m3. Prepared root zone material placed in one layer, accurately trimmed to design grades, finished with screeding batten and thoroughly consolidated using 3 passes of a vibrating plate compactor. Finished landform to be inspected and approved prior to turfing.

Rev A (9/05/03) AS-BUILT
Root-zone material mix ammended to suit site topsoil

National Galleries of Scotland

Construction detail 19
Landform construction

March 2001

Landform

Job no 989

Scale 1/20

Ian White Associates
Landscape Architects & Planners
3A Forrest Road, Stirling, FK8 1UH
Tel 01786 446 446 Fax 01786 446 441

Fig. 3.52 page 46: "Finished Level and Grades Plan", prepared by the landscape architecture office Ian White Associates.

Fig. 3.53 page 47: Typical cross sections, prepared by the landscape architecture office Ian White Associates.

Fig. 3.54 left: Typical construction detail, prepared by the landscape architecture office Ian White Associates.

Fig. 3.55 top: Landform under construction showing the formwork for the water edging.

Fig. 3.56 center: Landform during the site grading.

Fig. 3.57 bottom: Landform under construction showing the laying of the turf rolls.

Landform

In geography, landform describes the different formations of the earth's surface. These can be divided into three main categories: convex, concave, and flat landforms. The inclines of convex forms fall from an apex, flat, or lineal area to the surrounding terrain. A hilltop is one example. The inclines of concave forms run down towards a surface, line or point, as seen from the surrounding terrain. A depression is a typical concave form. Small flattenings-out can disrupt the inclines of both landform types. The term flat includes landforms with only minimal gradient.

The three coordinates x, y, z define the landforms described above. A suitable graphic code is needed in order to represent three-dimensional information in a two-dimensional map. Isohypses (contour lines) are used in topographical maps for this purpose. The name originates from the Greek *iso*, meaning equal, and *hypsos*, meaning height. Contour lines run along the landform and refer to sea level. They are separated by a constant interval, called the "equidistance". For unpracticed map readers, contours are often only a distracting tangle of lines. However, once the observer has a bit of practice, contour lines open up a huge reservoir of information.

Having made a few successful contour line interpretations, the map's landscape can be automatically visualized in the mind's eye. The next step is to verbally define the discovered shapes so that information can be exchanged about them. Unfortunately, this is where we encounter our next problem. It is not only in daily language that terms for the diversity of existing landforms are used with great imprecision. One important reason why such a multitude of terms exists may be that up to now no general standard work has been established itself in the field of landform terminology.

Dr. Georg Schulz has undertaken a step towards improvement with his book *Lexikon zur Bestimmung der Geländeformen in Karten* (Lexicon

for Identifying Landforms in Maps). In contrast to other literature on map interpretation, the author limits himself to landform, providing 300 definitions with detailed slope, height, and size indications. He also provides an interpretation key for correct landform terminology.

A selection of landforms is presented on the following pages. These examples have been selected as they are both particularly common in continental Europe and didactically suitable for learning about contour interpretation. In each ease, a contour map is compared with the corresponding three-dimensional terrain model. The brief explanations about the individual shapes and the digital models correlate with the principles clarified in Schulz's book. There is no space here for an exhaustive exposition on the extensive field of landform. For this, we strongly recommend the above-mentioned work.

Fig. 4.1 left: Drumlin landscape near Menzingen in Canton Zug (convex).

Fig. 4.2 right: Volcano in southern Italy (concave).

Fig. 4.3 bottom: The Linth flats near Weesen (flat).

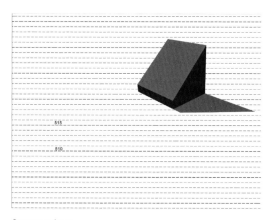

Constant slope

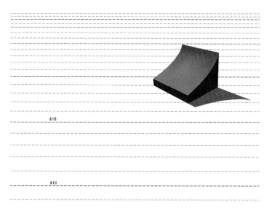

Fig. 4.4: Constant slope
With a constant slope the gradient is more or less the same over the entire area of inclination. In a topographical map, the constant slope is shown by consecutive parallel contour lines at an equal distance from one another.

Concave slope

Fig. 4.5: Concave slope
A slope is defined as concave when it possesses a curve negative to the earth's mid-point. This basic form is shown in maps in the characteristic pattern of contour lines which are initially far apart but with increasing elevation become closer.

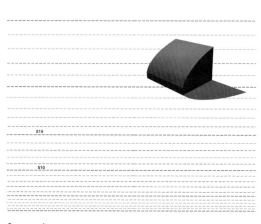

Fig. 4.6: Convex slope
As the reverse shape of the concave slope, the curve of the convex slope is positive. On the map, this slope form is recognizable in the contour lines which are increasingly far apart with increasing height.

Convex slope

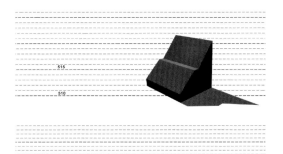

Terrace

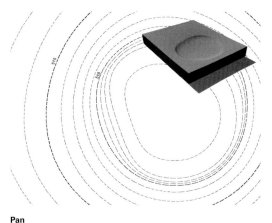

Pan

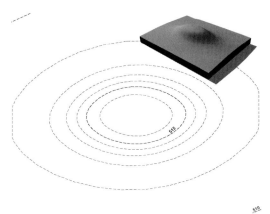

Knoll

Fig. 4.7: Terrace
A terrace is a flattening-out, which interrupts the uniform inclination of a slope. A terrace is composed of the terrace flat, the uphill slope lying above it, and the downhill slope below. When a slope is composed of many terraces on top of one another, it is described as terraced.

Fig. 4.8: Pan
A pan is an extremely flat, round depression, with slowly rising inclinations around the circumference. The extent of its surface is many times that of its difference in elevation.

Fig. 4.9: Knoll
In plan view, knolls are round; in profile they are a bell-shaped rise. The sides of a knoll are convex and radially abut the flattened summit area.

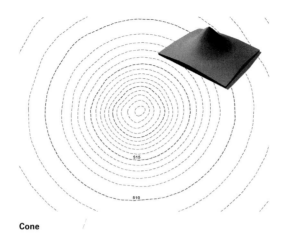

Cone

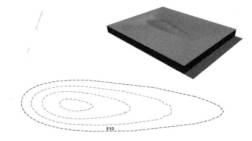

Fig. 4.10: Cone
Cones are practically circular in plan, with the sides varying from elliptical to concave. They are centrally tapered and of various sizes.

Drumlin

Fig. 4.11: Drumlin
The term "drumlin" refers to an elongated elliptical hill with a width to length ratio of 1 : 4. They are found in glacial landscapes, where the longitudinal axis lies in the direction of the glacial action. This landform resembles a droplet in shape.

Fig. 4.12: Basin
A basin is a roundish, concave landform with gently rising sides. These shallow and usually concave side slopes surround the flat basin floor on all sides.

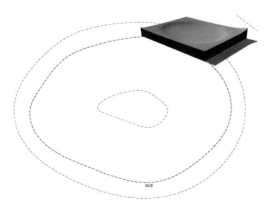

Basin

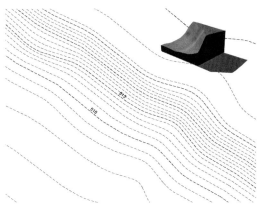

Cuesta

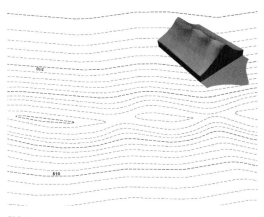

Shoulder

Fig. 4.13: Cuesta
The term "cuesta" refers to a steep escarpment formed through the erosion of different rock layers. A flat, gently sloped plateau, with a slope that corresponds to the underlying geological strata, is found at the top of the long extended escarpment.

Fig. 4.14: Shoulder
A shoulder, like a ridge, is a long, high-altitude area that slopes down on two sides like a roof. But unlike the mountain ridge, the sides of a mountain shoulder are convex in shape when seen in cross section. Changes in elevation along the ridge line are significantly less than the changes in elevation of the side inclines.

Fig. 4.15: Ridge
Ridge defines an extended mountain edge where the two sides fall downwards from the ridge line like a roof. Changes in elevation along the ridge are less than in the cross section. If the ridge is already strongly eroded, convex, rounded dome forms are present. In contrast to a shoulder, the ridge cross section line is straight to gently concave as it tapers up to its crest.

Ridge

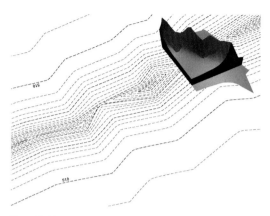

Summit ridge

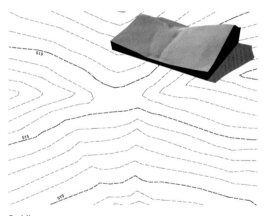

Fig. 4.16: Summit ridge
The summit ridge has a sharply formed ridge line with side inclines that fall away steeply, and are usually concave in cross section. Differences in elevation along the ridge are significantly less than those in the cross section.

Saddle

Fig. 4.17: Saddle
The term "saddle" defines an indentation in a mountain ridge. In longitudinal section, a saddle appears as a basin-like depression.

Fig. 4.18: Spur
A spur is a long, narrow projection jutting out from a bigger, convex landform.

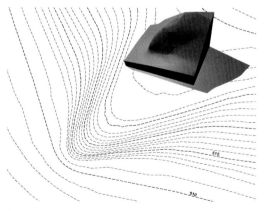

Spur

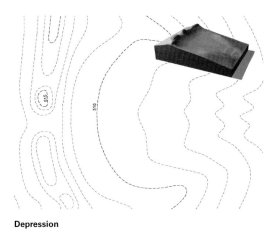

Depression

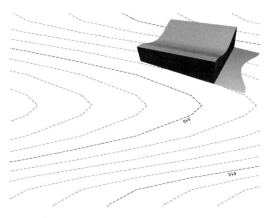

Basin valley

Fig. 4.19: Depression
A depression is a flat and wide hollow, which lies at the beginning of a valley. In cross section it is basin-like, whereas in plan it is not completely surrounded by rises. Unevenness on the depression floor is characteristic.

Fig. 4.20: Basin valley
A basin valley is a valley shape with a basin-like cross section. The sides and valley floor are concave, whereas the sides may have a lightly convex top. The longitudinal section features a long, extended concave shape with an even slope.

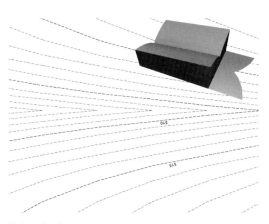

V-shaped valley

Fig. 4.21: V-shaped valley
A V-shaped valley is a broad concave landform with steep V-shaped or rounded valley walls in cross section. The valley floor is largely the same as that of a water body. The longitudinal section gradient is even.

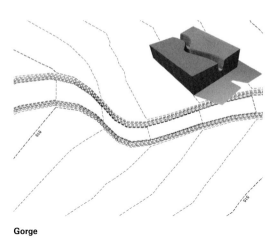

Gorge

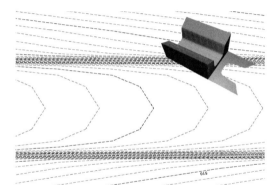

U-shaped valley

Fig. 4.22: Gorge
A gorge is the typical steep
canyon of mountain regions.
Its cross section shows very
steep, and sometimes even
overhanging walls. The valley
floor of the gorge is completely occupied by a river.

Fig. 4.23: U-shaped valley
A U-shaped valley is a valley
transformed by glacial action. Its lower sections have
a U-shaped cross section,
and its upper sections are
V-shaped.

Fig. 4.24: Braided river valley
The braided river valley is
a long, extended, concave
landform. The cross section
reveals a wide flat floodplain,
which is home to a meander-
ing river bed. The bordering
hillsides are convex.

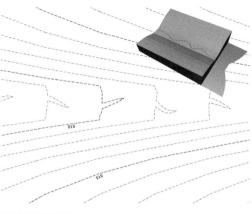

Braided river valley

Landform and landscape architecture

Fig. 4.25 top: Spurs in a garden in the National Garden Festival (Bundesgartenschau) in Munich, 2005.

Fig. 4.26 center: Depression shapes in a Japanese garden.

Fig. 4.27 bottom: Cone shapes in a hotel garden in Guatemala.

Site Grading 101

"Practice makes perfect" is a phrase which readily applies to site grading. The following pages will familiarize you with some of the basics. Exercises at the back of the book will help you put into practice everything you learn in this chapter.

Small and Large Scale

The terms "large scale" and "small scale" frequently come up during project meetings. Have you noticed that many professionals actually use these terms incorrectly in terms of their cartographical meaning? Plan drawings are the basic tool of a designer: so listen up, architects, engineers, landscape architects and other designers! Scale was first used in cartography and drawn in maps before anyone had even dreamt of zoning or detail design plans. It is therefore cartography that provides the correct definition of large and small scale – a definition that should be used both verbally and in writing.

Scale describes the relationship between two points on a map (or plan) and the actual distance in nature. For example, a scale of 1:100 means that one unit on the plan corresponds to 100 units of the same size in nature. The bigger the scale, the closer it approaches actual size. Plans with a small scale (meaning a larger number) show more parts of a project. They are less detailed than large-scale plans. Thus, a plan of 1:10 is larger-scale than a plan of 1:100.

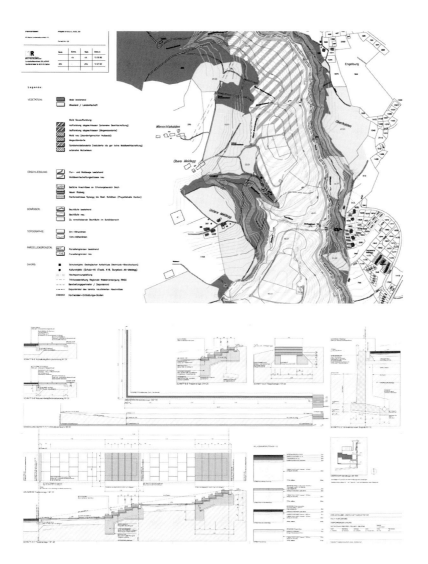

Put simply, the rule is:

large scale = small area, small scale = large area.

Typical scales for construction documents are:

1:1 – 1:5 – 1:10 – 1:20 – 1:50 – 1:100.

Typical scales for site grading are:

1:100 – 1:200 – 1:500 – 1:1000.

Fig. 5.1: Land use plan, scale 1: 5000 – small scale. (The scale correlates to the original drawing).

Fig. 5.2: Detail drawings scale 1:10/20/50 – large scale. (The scale correlates to the original drawing).

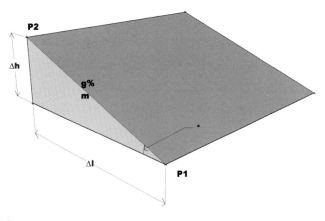

Slope

What is the difference between grade, slope, ratio and angle of re-pose? Generally speaking, there is none. These terms are different ways of defining an inclination. A bit more clarity will be shed on this terminology below.

Slope Calculations in Percent

Mathematicians speak of slope, which is represented using the letter m. In the Cartesian coordinate system, which uses a horizontal x-axis and vertical y-axis, the two points P1 and P2 are defined in coordinates as follows:

$$P1 = (x1,y1) \quad P2 = (x2,y2)$$

The grade of the line connecting points P1 and P2 can be calculated using the following formula:

$$m = \frac{(y_1 - y_2)}{(x_1 - x_2)} = \frac{difference\ in\ y}{difference\ in\ x}$$

Water needs a gradient to drain from plazas, paths and built structures, which is why landscape architects always speak of gradient. As in slope, gradient is denoted as g, the ratio between Δh, the height difference between two points, and Δl, the distance or length between two points. The value g is multiplied by 100 to obtain gradient as a percentage.

Fig. 5.3: Slope in percent, ratio and angle.

$$g = \Delta h{:}\Delta l$$
$$g\% = g \times 100$$

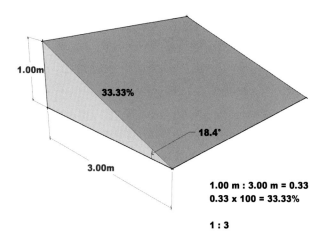

1.00 m : 3.00 m = 0.33
0.33 x 100 = 33.33%

1 : 3

These two conversion formulae are very useful:

$$\Delta l = \Delta h{:}g$$
$$\Delta h = g \times \Delta l$$

Ratio

The gradient of a hill can be denoted as a ratio. The height difference is given before, and the horizontal distance after the colon. Common ratios are: 1:1, 1:2, 1:3, 2:3.

1: 1	= 100%	1:8.3	= 12%
1: 1.5	= 66.6%	1:10	= 10%
1: 2	= 50%	1:12.5	= 8%
1: 2.5	= 40%	1:16.5	= 6 %
1: 3	= 33.3%	1:20	= 5%
1: 4	= 25%	1:5	= 4%
1: 5	= 20%	1:33.3	= 3%
1: 6	= 16.6%	1:50	= 2%
1: 6.6	= 15%	1:100	= 1%

Fig. 5.4: A sample calculation for gradient in percent.

Table 1: Ratios and their percent gradient.

63

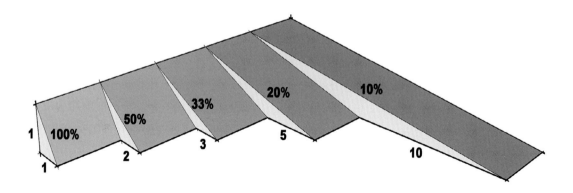

Angle of Incline

The angle of incline of a plane can be calculated based on the x-axis. In civil engineering this is termed "embankment angle" and can be used to compute earthwork calculations for the design of dams, road embankments, construction trenches and utility trenches. The angle of incline is calculated as:

$$tan\ (ß) = opposite\ /\ adjacent\ and\ tan\ (ß) = g\ and\ ß = arctan\ (g)$$

Angle of incline for the most important grade ratios:

1 : 3	=	18.4°
1 : 2	=	26.6°
1 : 1.5	=	33.7°
2 : 3	=	33.7°
1 : 1	=	45.0°

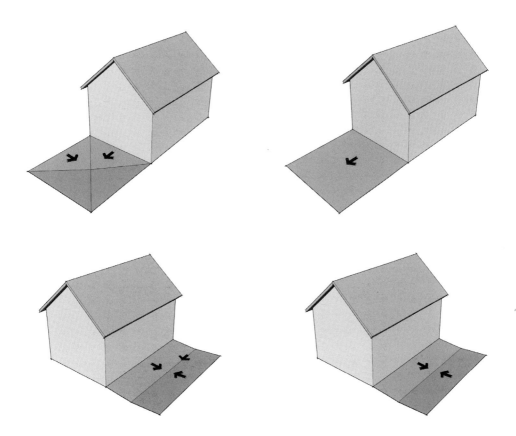

Gradient Formations

Three forms of gradient are possible for hardscape drainage:
— funneled slope
— pitched slope
— reversed pitched with or without fall

Hipped roof slopes, reversed funnels and reversed roofs are drainage forms that do not commonly occur in hardscape drainage.

The following profile types describe roads and paths:

— Soft crown
— Sharp crown
— Pitched slope

Fig. 5.6 top left: Funneled slope to a single lowpoint.

Fig. 5.7 top right: Pitched slope with a single plane.

Fig. 5.8 bottom left: Reverse pitch with longitudinal fall.

Fig. 5.9 bottom right: Reverse pitch without longitudinal fall.

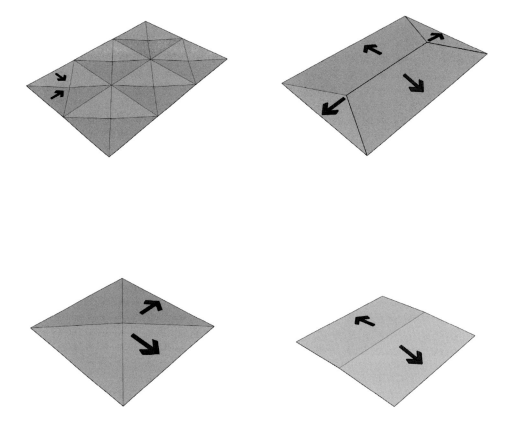

Fig. 5.10 top left: Hard-scape surface with several funnel drains and multiple lowpoints.

Fig. 5.11 top right: Hipped roof slope.

Fig. 5.12 center left: Reverse funnel slope with a single highpoint.

Fig. 5.13 center right: Pitched slope without fall.

Fig. 5.14 bottom: Road profiles: pitched slope, sharp crown, soft crown.

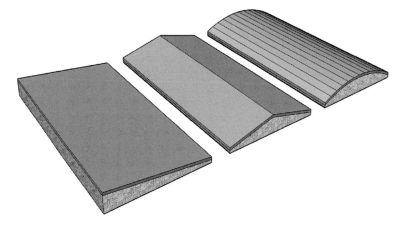

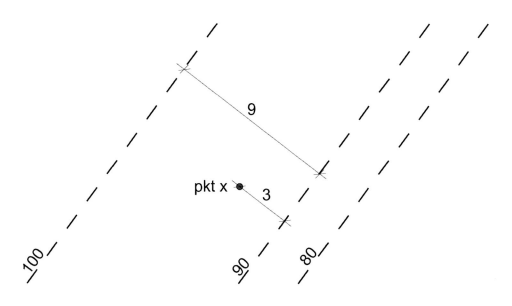

Interpolation

Interpolation is based on the ratio of part elevation to total elevation equalling that of part distance to total distance. Or put more simply, part to the whole. Manual interpolation used to be the chief method used to create contour maps. A uniform grid was laid out on site, and elevations were taken. The grid and elevation readings were then transferred onto a scaled plan and, using interpolation points of identical elevation, were connected, creating the contour map. Several digital methods now replace this onerous process.

Instead of calculating slope, interpolation provides an elegant method of finding out the elevation of a point between two contour lines. In the example below, we want to discover the elevation of point x.

Using the formula, the ratio part distance: total distance equals part elevation: total elevation, we can quickly determine the elevation of the point.

Fig. 5.15:
part distance = 3,
total distance = 9,
total change in elevation = 10

part elevation = x

3: 9 = x: 10 or x = 3.33

Spot elevation = 93.33 m.

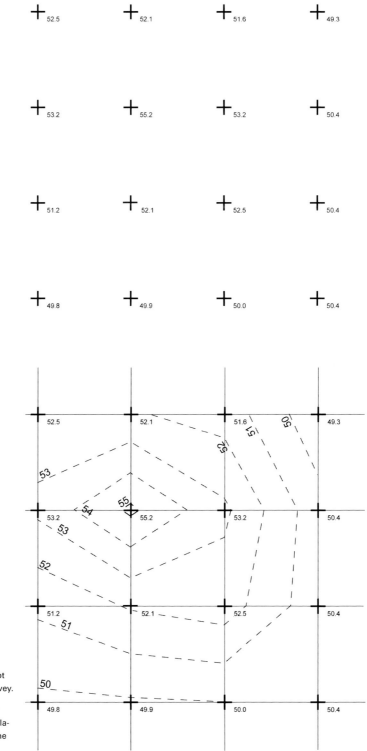

Fig. 5.16 top: Grid and spot
elevations from a site survey.

Fig. 5.17 bottom: Contour
map based on the interpolation of elevations along the
grid lines.

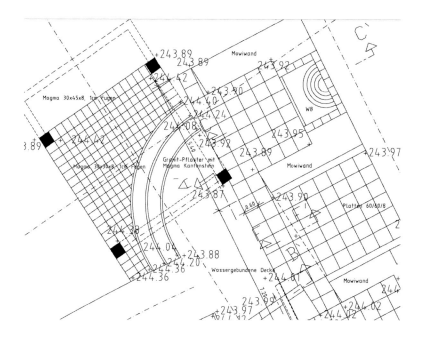

Spot Elevations

You will not get far on a construction site using contour lines, because you need spot elevations to get things built! For paths and plazas, spot elevations should be shown at intersections, junctions, buildings, high-points and lowpoints. A "+" or "x" to the left of the number indicates the exact location of the spot elevation in the grading plan. Conversely, an equilateral triangle is commonly used in sections, elevations and pro-files. Depending on the level of precision required, the spot elevations are shown with two to three decimal places, and normally refer to mean sea level. In Germany, the reference datum is the sea level at Amsterdam, and since the end of the 1990s the abbreviation NHN has been used for normal zero level. In Austria, an average value for the Adriatic at Triest is used and is abbreviated m.ü.Adria. Switzerland and the Principality of Lichtenstein use meters above sea level (m.ü.M.), referring to the sea level at Marseille. Small construction projects may use a local spot elevation as a reference point (for example, a manhole cover, the house entrance and so forth). All other elevations are then given relative to this point. To avoid negative elevations, professional literature recommends using a number with a high, rounded value, for example H = 100 (see Lehr 2003). Particular care should be paid to building entrances as the given elevations can be for either finished or unfinished floor levels. Geographers use the term "invert level" instead of spot elevation.

Fig. 5.18: Spot elevations are needed to get things built, not contour lines.

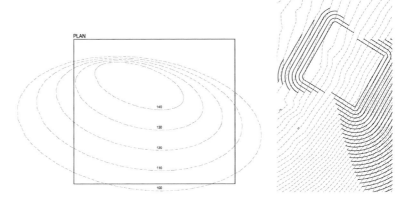

PLAN

Contour Lines

Contour lines are the best method for representing three-dimensional landforms in two dimensions on a map or drawing. Contours are also very effective for indicating proposed changes to a project area. Imagine you are to design a golf course. It is basically impossible to visualize the design using only spot elevations, whereas with contour lines one can quickly gain a spatial impression of the concept. For landscape architects, contour lines are *the* tool for visualizing and manipulating outdoor spaces.

A contour line connects points of the same elevation. The elevation of a given point refers to a reference benchmark or datum. For maps and plans, the reference datum is generally mean sea level. The term isohypse is also used to indicate contour lines. In contrast, isobaths indicate underwater depth lines. The shorelines of puddles, ponds and lakes are visible as contour lines in the landscape. Contour lines are drawn in scale and shown at regular equidistances (intervals) on topographic maps and plans. To improve readability, main contour lines can be shown using lines of greater thickness to differentiate from contour lines of only secondary importance.

Contour lines should always be labeled. The base of the elevation label sits on or between the contours with its base orientated downhill. If the interval between contours is known (for example, 1 meter, 5 meters, 10 meters), a single contour elevation given on the plan is enough to clearly define in which direction the terrain rises or falls.

Existing contours are always dashed; proposed contours are drawn with a continuous line. Both existing and proposed contours should be shown in design and construction drawings, and thus both line types should be present.

The perpendicular line between two contour lines is the shortest distance and consequently also has the greatest slope. Water always takes

Fig. 5.19 left: Contour lines are always closed; but this may not always be shown within the plan area.

Fig. 5.20 right: Proposed contours are shown with a continuous and thicker line, and existing contours are always dashed. This grading concept requires cut and fill.

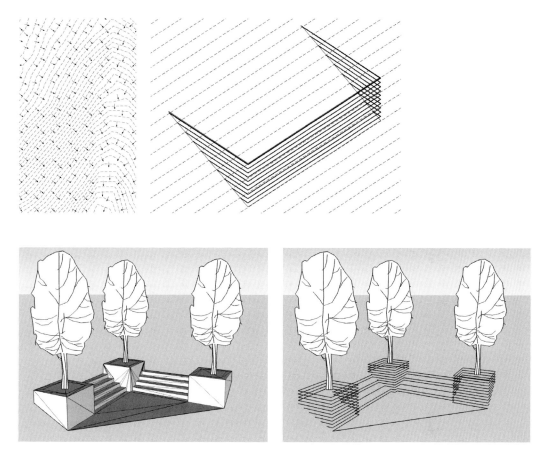

the fastest and steepest route downhill, consequently water flows at right angles to contour lines.

Contour lines are continuous and represent a closed shape, possibly shown within the extent of the drawing or not. Accordingly, a single, unclosed contour line cannot lie within closed contour lines. If we want to show highpoints or lowpoints using contours, the lines will either be closed (even if this occurs outside the limits of the drawing) or run parallel. Contour lines never split. Overlapping only occurs when overhangs are depicted.

Spot elevations can be used in addition to contours to indicate changes of elevation between contour lines. If no spot elevations are present, we can assume a uniform and consistent gradient between contour lines. The base line connects the points at which the proposed contour lines meet the existing ones.

Fig. 5.21 top left: Arrows show the direction of water flow.

Fig. 5.22 top right: The proposed contour lines of a retaining wall run along the wall face.

Fig. 5.23 bottom left: A shaded model of steps.

Fig. 5.24 bottom right: The contour lines run at even intervals along the steps.

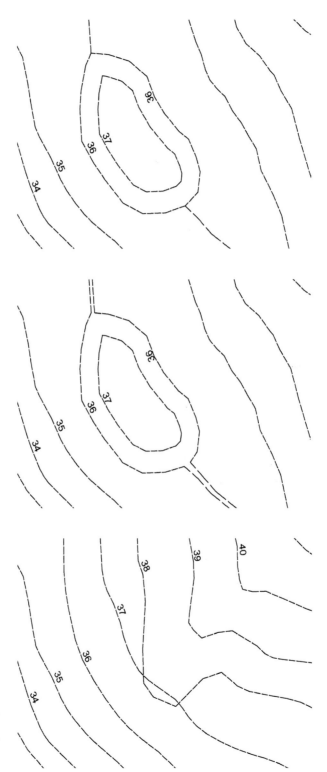

Fig. 5.25 top: Contour lines never split into two lines.

Fig. 5.26 center: Instead of splitting, they run parallel to each other, even when separated by only a very small distance.

Fig. 5.27 bottom: Contour lines cross only when showing the difference between existing and proposed grading or to show an overhang as here.

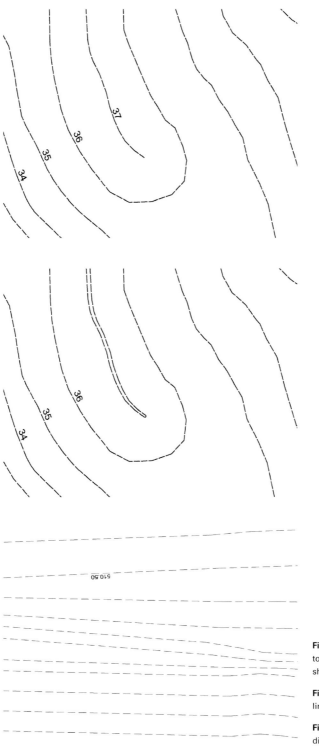

Fig. 5.28 top: A single contour line that just stops, as shown here, is not possible.

Fig. 5.29 center: Contour lines are always closed.

Fig. 5.30 bottom: In which direction does the terrain rise?

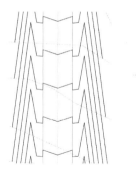

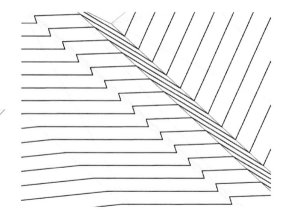

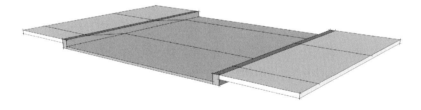

Fig. 5.31 top left: Contour line layout of a section of road with a curb.

Fig. 5.32 top center: The road profile.

Fig. 5.33 top right: The contour lines run up the edge of the curb until reaching an elevation where they can run back into the surroundings.

Fig. 5.34 bottom: The run of the contour lines for a sloped road with a curb.

The layout of contour lines along a curb always appears at first glance to be somewhat complicated. The trick is to systematically calculate spot elevations along the axis. The best way is to start in the middle of the road and draw a y-axis (dashed line) and an x-axis (dot-dashed). The long and cross gradients are defined through arrows and notations. Once the elevations have been worked out along the y-axis, switch to the x-axis and calculate the elevations there. Points of the same elevation produce a profile that can be repeatedly copied if the gradient remains constant along the road.

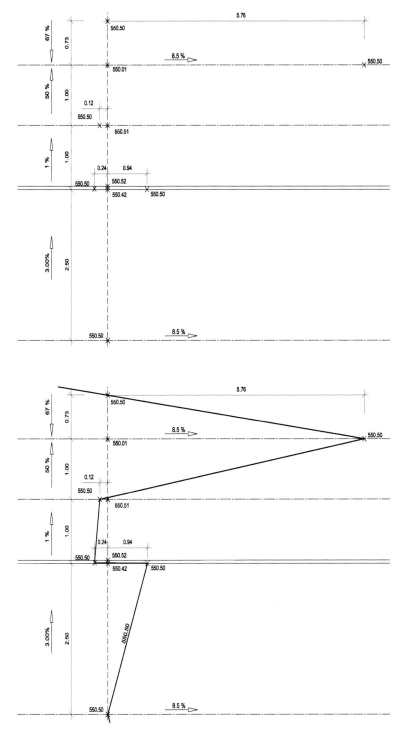

Fig. 5.35 top: Road detail with a 10 cm curb, 8.5% longitudinal gradient and a ditch on the side (with 1:2 and 2:3 embankments). Spot elevations are calculated for the x-axis (dot-dashed line) and y-axis (dashed line).

Fig. 5.36 bottom: Contour plan of the road with spot elevations and contours.

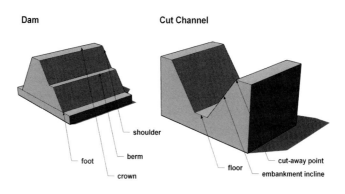

Fig. 5.37: A dam and channel embankment.

Embankments

A hill is a naturally sloped landform. If a mound is created artificially, it is called an embankment. Embankment forms include dams (filled embankments), channels (cut embankments), and double profiles (half dam with fill, half channels with cut and side cut embankments). The embankment incline is given in degrees from the horizontal, slope ratio or percent slope. An embankment has a foot or lower edge, sides, and an upper edge. Drainage channels can be found below or above the embankment.

Berms are step-like subdivisions of the embankment. They have a width of 1 to 2.5 meters. Berms fulfill the following purposes:
— Decreasing the earth pressure on the embankment foot
— Access path for maintenance of the embankment
— Drainage for high embankments
— Anti-fall safety barrier
— Interception point for falling material

The embankment angle ß is the angle between the horizon of the ground and the line of the embankment. For example, dry sand has a natural angle of repose between 28 and 45°, depending on density, grain shape and particle size grading. Embankments with an angle of 2:3 (33.7°) are typical, and are considered stable. If the embankment angle is more than 33.7° (2:3 or 1:1.5) it is referred to as a steep slope. In this case, stabilization elements are generally necessary, as the proposed slope is greater than the natural angle of repose (ß).

Binding soils have a higher silt and clay content than other soils. This additional cohesion indicates the ability of the soil particles to bind to one another. If the cohesion of the soil is very high, the embankment angle may exceed the natural angle of repose.

Embankment angle ß for the most important gradient ratios:

1 : 3   ß = 18.4°
1 : 2   ß = 26.6°
1 : 1.5 ß = 33.7°
2 : 3   ß = 33.7°
1 : 1   ß = 45.0°

Profile

A profile is the side view of the earth's surface taken along a given plane. In contrast to a section, which includes information about the inner make-up of the cut object, a profile gives information about the surface alone.

Profiles are drawn to scale based on the plan view. The elevations of the profile plan are commonly enlarged by a factor of ten to make the elevation differences more pronounced. The vertical increase is expressed as follows:

Vertical exaggeration = horizontal scale / vertical scale

Fig. 5.38 top left: The natural angle of repose of gravel.

Fig. 5.39 top right: Embankment lower edge, drainage channel, and embankment upper edge, the Garden terraces of Haifa, Israel.

Table 3: Grade ratios and correlating embankment angles.

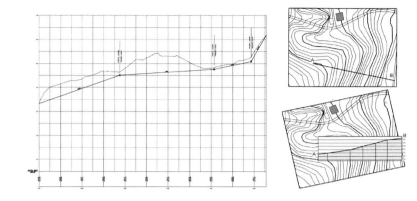

For example, a profile with an exaggeration of 10:1 has a horizontal scale of 1:1000 and a vertical scale of 1:100.

Longitudinal profiles of roadway alignments are based on the central axis of the road. This line is defined as a gradient and is broken into 20 meter sections. The sections are called stations, and often start with the station 0 + 000.000 = 0 kilometers.

A technical profile drawing should always include the following:
— Reference elevation
— Profile number
— Scale (scale exaggeration, where relevant)
— Existing elevations
— Proposed elevations
— Horizontal and vertical stations, for example 0+25
— Changes in direction

To prepare a profile manually, the following steps are necessary:
1. Connect two points on a map with a line
2. Define the highest and lowest points
3. Label and draw horizontal elevation lines on the new profile drawing
4. Orientate the map to the profile drawing
5. Draw perpendicular lines from the contour line to its relevant horizontal line on the profile drawing
6. Connect the points of intersections, creating the profile.

Fig. 5.40 left: Digital longitudinal profile of a proposed stream with a vertical exaggeration of 10:1.

Fig. 5.41 right: Manual preparation of a profile.

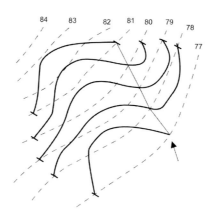

Cut and Fill Calculations

How much does it cost to remove a cubic meter of soil? The operator of a Swiss landfill charges CHF 7.50 per clean tonne of soil material. The specific weight of a cubic meter of spoil is 1.8 tonnes, making the disposal costs of a cubic meter of excavation material CHF 13.50 (€8.50 or about $12). If the cut material can be reused on site for fill, i.e. no soil needs to be transported to or from the site, we refer to balanced cut and fill. It is always worth trying to balance out the cut and fill to keep costs down.

Volume Calculations Using Profiles

A trapezoid is a geometric shape with a parallel base and top. A road can be thought of in terms of a series of trapezoids. The trapezoid formula is a helpful method of calculating the volume of long objects. It is assumed that the terrain runs straight from profile to profile. The profiles are parallel to one another and are always at a constant distance of d. A_1 and A_2 indicate the profile surface areas. The surface area of an intended profile in the middle is called A_m. Using this data, the volume between the profiles can be calculated.

$$\text{Trapezoid formula: } V = \frac{d}{6} \cdot (A_1 + 4A_m + A_2)$$

The area between the first and last profile and the existing terrain are remainders and their volume can be calculated using the following formula:

$$V = \frac{d}{2} \cdot A$$

Fig. 5.42: The base line connects the points where proposed and existing contour lines intersect. This is an example of balanced cut and fill. The base line also functions as the axis beyond which the cut material can be dumped in the fill area.

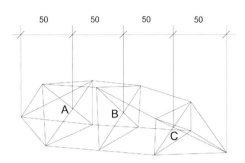

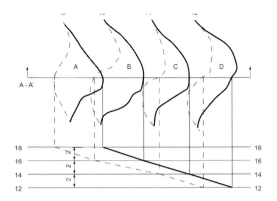

To calculate the surface of A_m, the corner points between the correlating points of the adjacent cross section need to be averaged. As this is an awkward calculation, the following approximation formula is used instead. Both remainder volumes are included:

$$V = d \cdot \left(\frac{A_1}{2} + \frac{A_1 + A_2}{2} + \frac{A_2}{2} \right)$$

Volume Calculations Using Contour Lines

This is perhaps the quickest method of determining volumes, as we need only a plan and do not need to generate profile drawings. Nevertheless, a correct set of existing and proposed contour lines is essential. In principle, volume calculation using contour lines relates directly to volume calculation using profiles. The interval between the contour lines corresponds to the distance between profiles; the surface area between the existing and new contour lines is one such profile. The above-mentioned trapezoid formula can therefore be employed.

Most data are now available in digital form. Using the surface area tools that every CAD-program has, surface area measurements are quickly obtained. In the past, designers and engineers used planimeters. Where large earthworks are involved, a digital site model with volume calculation commands is the most effective solution.

Fig. 5.43 left: Calculation of earth volumes using the approximation formula:

$V = 50 \cdot \left(\frac{A}{2} + \frac{A+B}{2} + \frac{B+C}{2} + \frac{C}{2} \right)$

Fig. 5.44 right: Example of volume calculation from contour lines using the approximation formula:

$V = 2 \cdot \left(\frac{A}{2} + \frac{A+B}{2} + \frac{B+C}{2} + \frac{C+D}{2} + \frac{D}{2} \right)$

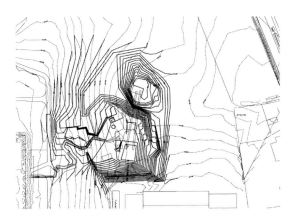

Grading: Purpose and Techniques

The Purpose of Site Grading

Every landscape architectural project, regardless of whether it is a big development or small domestic garden, deals with changes of the site's surface. A good, restrained grading concept will determine whether a project is successful or not. Too little gradient and water will puddle, possibly penetrating into built structures and causing frost and meltwater damage. Conversely, overly steep gradients can lead to landslides and soil erosion, both of which can cause enormous damage.

We all know projects with buildings, roads and other infrastructure that are poorly integrated into the landscape. Integration, or rather accentuation through site and vegetation, improves landscape character. The three main focuses of site grading are:

Creating Level Space

Seating areas, parking lots and sports facilities all need level space. The term level is not totally correct. Naturally, these level spaces also have an internal grade so that water can drain away.

Circulation

Roads and paths connect point A to point B. Roads and paths generally have slopes. Embankments are used to create an interface with the existing site. Standard gradients for roads and pavements as set down in building and engineering codes should be observed.

Fig. 5.45: Digital contour model of the project Ravensburg Playland, Phase III. Design: Rotzler Krebs Partner Landscape Architects BSLA. Digital contour model: Peter Petschek.

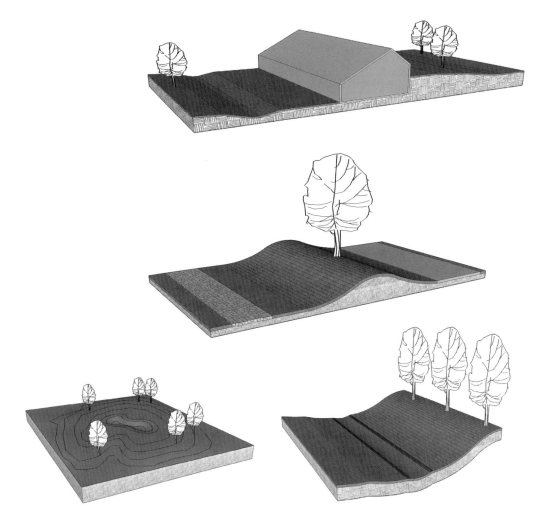

Fig. 5.46 top: Creating level space for a building using site grading.

Fig. 5.47 center: Site grading is always part of designing circulation.

Fig. 5.48 bottom: Depressions and swales can serve both as design elements and water infiltration infrastructure.

Natural Grading

Geometric or naturally landscaped hills, swales and depressions create accents. They are important design elements in landscape architecture. The task of collecting and infiltrating rain water in depressions without outlets (hollows) and open ditches with a slight gradient (swales) has gained increasing importance in recent years.

Fig. 5.49 top: A level seating area.

Fig. 5.50 center: Accessing a lookout hill via a path graded into the site.

Fig. 5.51 bottom: Natural site grading with a swale and hollow for rainwater infiltration.

Important Criteria

There are many important criteria that need to be kept in mind while developing a grading concept. The most important points to ensure functioning site grading are:

1. The grading around buildings should always be orientated to fall away from the building.

2. Level areas with puddling water should never be allowed to occur.

3. Site grading extends only to the site boundaries.

4. The grading concept always starts with the elevations of existing buildings, roads or paths.

5. An initial grading concept on sketch paper with contour lines should be further developed in parallel with the overall design and drainage concept. The end result should be a grading and layout plan with existing and proposed contour lines, spot elevations, gradient indications, grade parting (crown) lines, and the layout of all important construction elements.

6. The maximum and minimum gradient of various surfaces must be observed (see the grading guidelines on the next page). Gradients of 4% and above are visible to the naked eye! A manual lawn mower can only be used on gradients up to 26.6° (1:2 or 50%). Manufacturers of ride-on mowers recommend a limit of 10° because of the ride-on's high center of gravity. Special mowers are used for steeper embankments.

7. Spot elevations should always be shown at the following locations:
   - corners of buildings, entrances to buildings
   - all corners of parking lots
   - terraces and other paved surfaces
   - at path/pavement intersections
   - at the top and bottom of steps and walls
   - drain inlets and high and lowpoints
   Spot elevations are more important than contour lines.

8. The extent of a tree crown is the line resulting from the vertical continuation of the edge of the tree's crown downward towards the ground. Trees require a protection area of the crown's extent plus 1.5 meters outward. No grading should ever take place within this area.

Table 4 right page: Gradient Standard Guidelines.

Minimum and Maximum Slope

Type	minimum slope in %	maximum slope in %
Roads / Pavement / Plazas		
road longitudinal gradient, 30 km/h speed limit	0.5%	12%
road cross gradient, 30 km/h speed limit	2%	7%
pedestrian path longitudinal gradient	–	10%
pedestrian path cross gradient	1%	4%
disabled access ramp	6%	8%
parking longitudinal gradient	1%	5%
parking cross gradient	1%	10%
seating area	1%	2%
service area	1%	8%
Planted Areas		
football field (competitive)	0.5%	1%
grass play area (non-competitive)	1%	5%
lawn	1%	25%
planting areas	0.5%	10%
embankments with normal soil	–	66%
embankments with poor soil	–	50%
drainage channels longitudinal gradient	1%	8%
drainage channels cross gradient	2%	25%
drainage swales cross gradient	2%	10%
Paving		
natural stone slabs and pavers, sawn / flamed	1%	
natural stone slabs and pavers, cleft	2%	
concrete slabs and pavers, sandblasted	1.5%	
exposed aggregate concrete slabs	2%	
in situ concrete, lightly structured	1.5%	
in situ concrete, rilled	2%	
crushed limestone/compacted chippings surfaces	1.5%	
grasscrete pavers	1.5%	
asphalt	1.5%	
protective matting surfaces	1.5%	

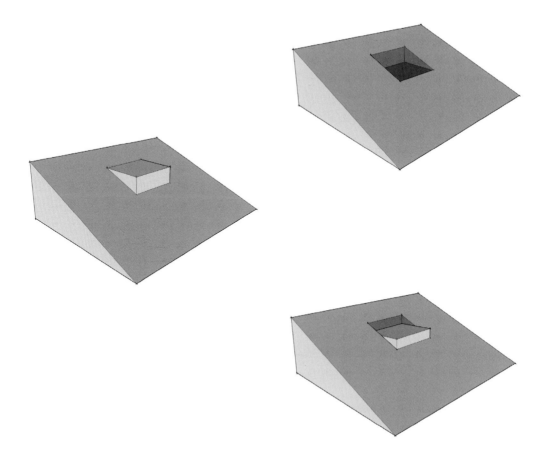

Site Grading and Buildings

The precise siting of architectural elements is a necessity. There are several ways in which the base of a building can be inserted into the terrain in relation to the existing site:

— As a cut

Fig. 5.52 top: Siting the building as cut.

— As a fill, with the foundations as the spatial edge

— As a combination of cut and fill.

Fig. 5.53 center: Siting the building as fill with the foundations as the spatial edge.

Fig. 5.54 bottom: Siting the building as a combination of cut and fill.

On balance, the pros and cons of each variation should be looked at in relation to the architectural expression of the building, its spatial and internal organization, circulation and so on. The overall effect of the building in the landscape is equally important.

Fig. 5.55 top: "Flarz", laborers' cottages in Beregg, Zurich Oberland.

Fig. 5.56 center: Farmer's house in the drumlin landscape near Menzingen, Canton Zug.

Fig. 5.57 bottom: Farmer's house in Oberegg, Etzel, Canton Schwyz.

Fig. 5.58 top: Alpe Foppa by Mario Botta, below Monte Tamaro in Canton Ticino.

Fig. 5.59 center: Housing development Neubühl in Zurich-Wollishofen (Architects: Haefeli, Moser, Roth, Steiger, Hubacher, Artaria, Schmidt. Landscape Architects: Ammann).

Fig. 5.60 bottom: Casa Bearth in Sumvitg, Canton Graubünden (Architects: Bearth & Deplazes Architekten AG).

Site Grading and Roads

Roadway alignments influence the character of a landscape. By comparing design alternatives as part of an environmental impact assessment, landscape architects are able to influence the effect of a road on landscape character. Landscape architects also participate in road projects by developing landscape maintenance plans. They also design entrances to hotels, clubs, and parking lots. This scope of activity demands a basic knowledge of roadway design, the key proponents of which can be transferred to pedestrian pathway design.

Basic Facts:
— 3.0 meters is the minimum width for a slow vehicular road.
— The longitudinal profile of a road should correlate sensibly with horizontal roadway alignment. Changes of direction after long straight sections should occur before and not after a hill.
— Road cuts are disadvantageous because of poor drainage and accumulation of snowdrifts.
— In flat areas a slight rise above the surrounding area should be aimed for (drainage, ground fog, snow), including a hard shoulder and embankment (1:4 to 1:5).
— Horizontal alignment, vertical alignment and a proposed cross section define a roadway design.

Fig. 5.61 left: A pass road in the Swiss Alps winds its way up the mountain.

Fig. 5.62 right: This trail is the fastest route to the top of the embankment but is not a suitable long-term solution.

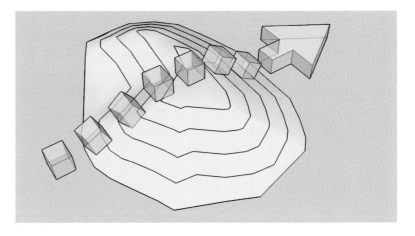

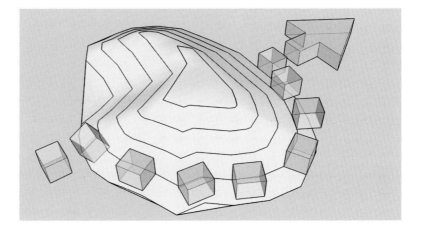

Fig. 5.63 top: A circulation route at right angles to the contour lines is the quickest route from A to B. However, above certain gradients, stepping or cuts will become necessary.

Fig. 5.64 bottom: A path or road that runs practically parallel to the contour lines takes longer to get from A to B, but requires no large-scale grading interventions.

— Simple axial curve geometry of tangent – curve – tangent is used for slow traffic. A tangent is defined as a line that is perpendicular to the radius of the curve at the point of intersection. Clothoid curves are used for faster-flowing traffic. These allow a continuous transition between straight and curved. Clothoid curves allow more even steering.

— Horizontal alignment: the minimum radius for a curve at a traffic speed of 30 km/h is 50 meters.

— Vertical alignment: the longitudinal gradient at a traffic speed of 30 km/h is maximum = 12%, minimum = 0.5%, the arc radius for hills / troughs should equal at least 2100 / 1200 meters.

— Cross section: maximum 7%, minimum 2%.

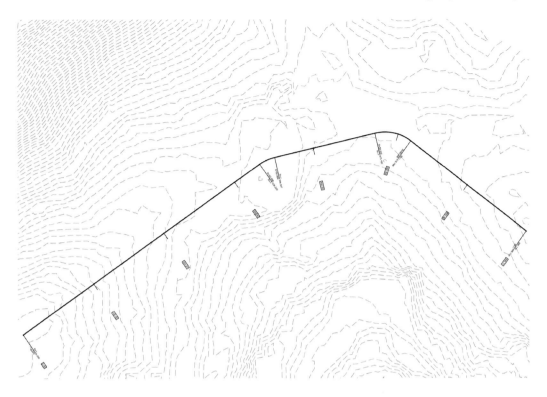

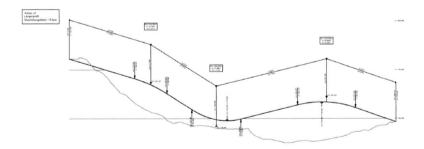

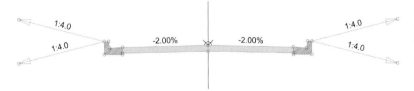

Fig. 5.65 top: A horizontal alignment with simple curve geometry.

Fig. 5.66 center: The vertical alignment shows two hills and one trough.

Fig. 5.67 bottom: A cross section of the road.

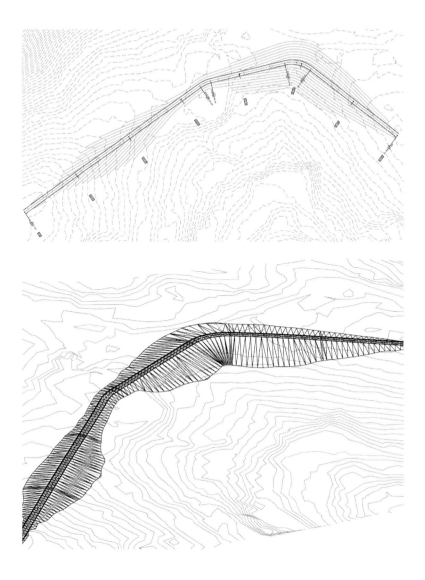

Fig. 5.68 top: The new road shown as a contour plan.

Fig. 5.69 bottom: Civil 3D site model of the new road.

Site Grading Approach: an Example

A terrace is to be constructed in a southwest-facing hillside. The terrace will have a finished elevation of 37.4 meters and should blend into the existing site with a gradient of 10%.

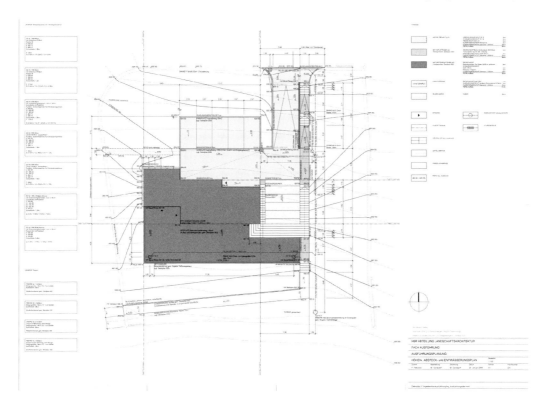

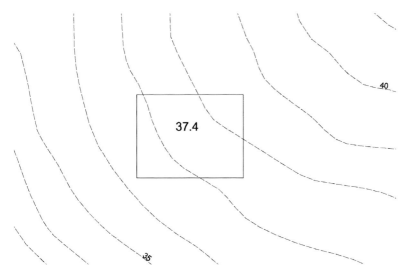

Fig. 5.70 top: Grading and drainage plan, drawn by a student of the University of Applied Sciences Rapperswil, 2005.

Fig. 5.71 bottom: The existing situation.

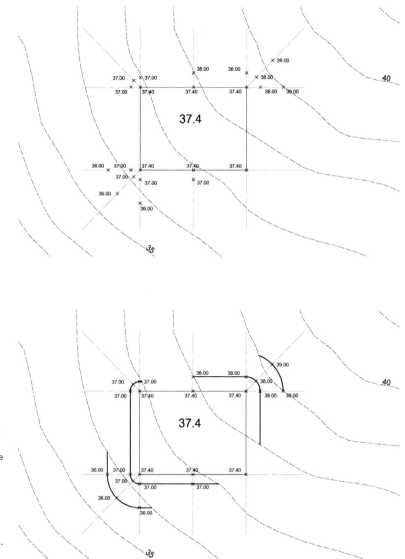

Fig. 5.72 top: First, the construction lines of the terrace are extended and the new elevations are computed. The conversion of the gradient formula is used: $\Delta l = \Delta h : g$.

Fig. 5.73 bottom: Once the new elevations have been entered on the plan, spot elevations of the same elevation are joined.

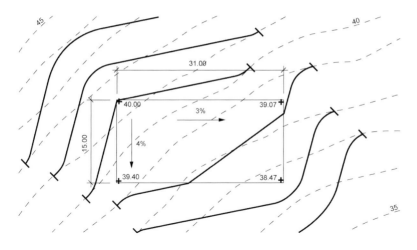

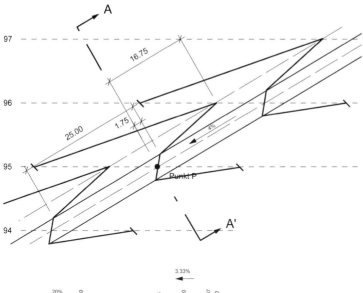

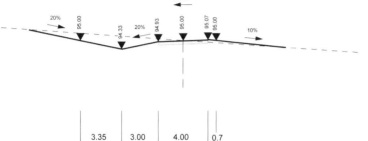

Fig. 5.74 top: The proposed task is to create a flat space: this area should be built as a gently sloped surface with both longitudinal and cross fall. The new area connects to the existing terrain with a slope of 15%.

Fig. 5.75: A road grading plan: starting from point P the contour lines are drawn based on the road profile shown below.

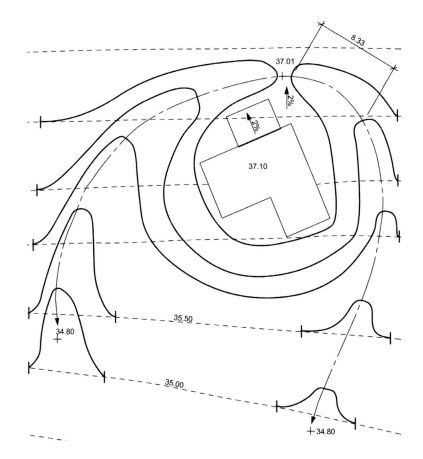

Fig. 5.76: Proposed task
natural stormwater grading:
swales convey water away
from the roof and parking
areas.

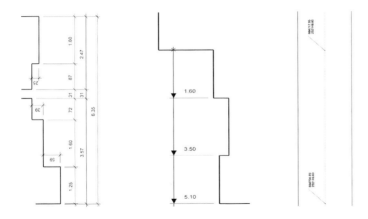

Grading and Layout Plan

A grading and layout plan are essential tools for transferring a design from the drawing onto the construction site. They provide scaled spatial definition in plan and elevation. Using the layout plan, the contractor should be able to stake out everything that is to be constructed on site.

The main purpose of the grading and layout plan is to give the appointed contractor a simple and precise overview of essential dimensions. The draftsperson must consider carefully which dimensions are necessary and which redundant. You should never double up on dimensions or provide too many. The intended communication of the plan is best achieved when the given dimensions are limited to less but more efficiently organized data.

The three most important dimensioning systems used in grading and layout plans are: chained (consecutive), running, and coordinate dimensioning.

It makes sense to differentiate between fixed, partially fixed, and flexible areas in the layout plan. Fixed elements such as buildings, site boundaries, or benchmarks are not dimensioned. They either already exist in the project area or will be erected at exactly the right spot. Proposed buildings are defined during construction using a tensioned line or marker pegs. The staking out by a surveyor provides the contractor with flight lines and the extents of the building. These days wire is used instead of line. Some contractors use theodolites or special surveying equipment (visiomats). Once the building has been erected, the surveyor returns to survey the building to update official records (property, cadastral, and local land survey). Naturally, this second mapping out is a good opportunity to check for any

Fig. 5.77 left: Chain dimensioning is the correct dimensioning style for building construction. It is composed of individual dimensions, part dimensions, and total dimensions.

Fig. 5.78: Running dimensioning is good for garden and landscape construction, as the numerical values never need to be calculated on site.

Fig. 5.79: Using easy-to-use total stations, non-surveyors can now also use coordinate dimensioning to stake out.

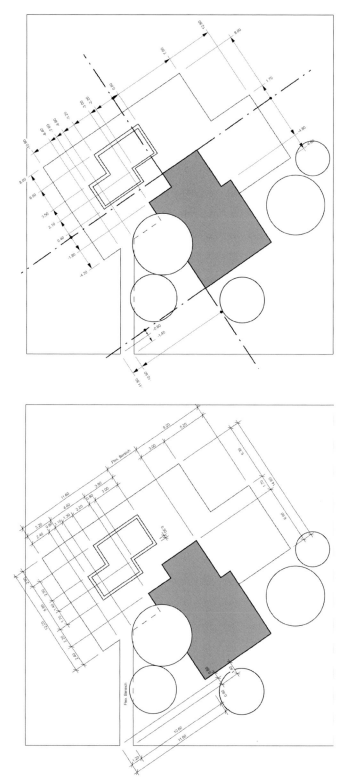

Fig. 5.80 top: Plan example of running dimensions.

Fig. 5.81 bottom: Plan example of chained (consecutive) dimensions.

mistakes, which fortunately occur only rarely. Walls, steps and trees can be staked out using the building marker stakes as a reference.

Partially fixed elements such as walls, steps and trees are referenced to building edges, boundary markers or coordinates. Three reference distances are always needed to localize an object. Fundamental landscape architecture elements such as paths, walls and steps can best be defined through a central axis with perpendicular width values.

Flexible areas and objects do not need dimensioning. For example, if the beginning or end of a path is clearly defined, a numerical value for its length would only add confusion.

Big earthworks projects, such as golf courses, or parks with large waterbodies and hills, need their own earthworks plans. Earthworks plans should always include an elevation grid. The grid size depends on the required grading and the scale of project. The following information should always be included in an earthworks plan:
— Existing elevations
— Proposed elevations
— The difference between the two

It should be decided in consultation with the contractor whether the shown elevations indicate finished levels or subgrade. In pre-construction documents, cut should be shown in yellow and fill in red.

Fig. 5.82: Stake out markers define the precise location of the building.

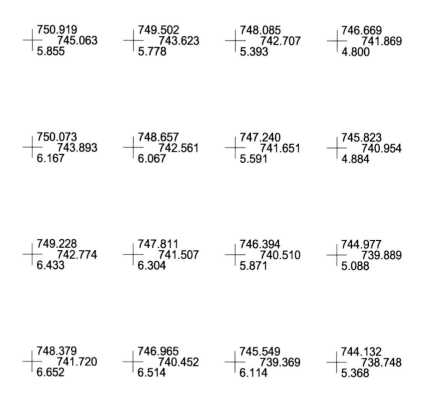

+ 750.919 745.063 5.855	+ 749.502 743.623 5.778	+ 748.085 742.707 5.393	+ 746.669 741.869 4.800
+ 750.073 743.893 6.167	+ 748.657 742.561 6.067	+ 747.240 741.651 5.591	+ 745.823 740.954 4.884
+ 749.228 742.774 6.433	+ 747.811 741.507 6.304	+ 746.394 740.510 5.871	+ 744.977 739.889 5.088
+ 748.379 741.720 6.652	+ 746.965 740.452 6.514	+ 745.549 739.369 6.114	+ 744.132 738.748 5.368

Fig. 5.83: Five-meter grid with existing elevations, proposed elevations, and the difference.

Fig. 5.84: Digital earth-works plan for Ravensburg Playland, Phase III. Design: Rotzler Krebs Partner Landscape Architects BSLA. Digital terrain model: Peter Petschek.

Fig. 5.85 right top: Grading and drainage plan, by a student of the University of Applied Sciences Rapperswil, 2006.

Fig. 5.86 right bottom: Grading and drainage plan, by a student of the University of Applied Sciences Rapperswil, 2007.

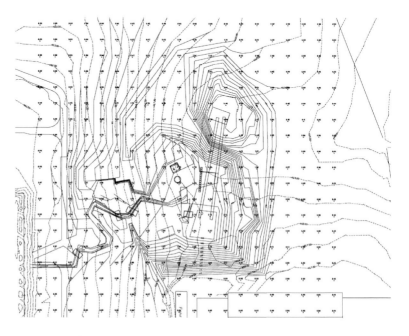

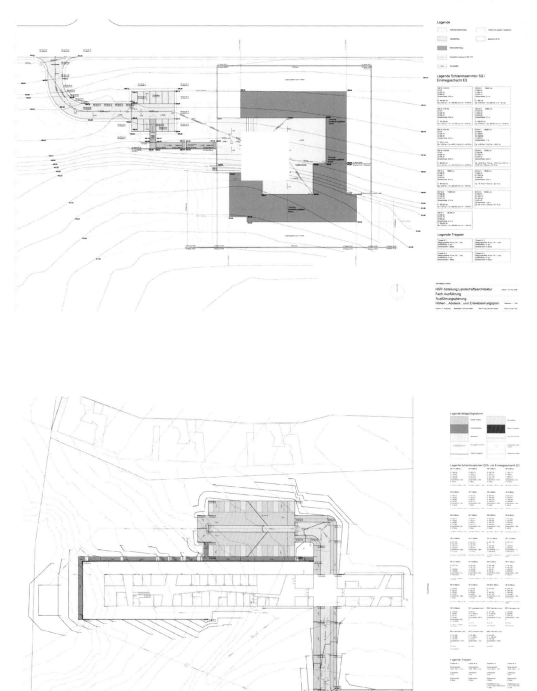

Stormwater Management and Site Grading

Stormwater Management Basics

Last summer, for the first time ever, a home hardware store ran a series of TV commercials showcasing rainwater recycling products. Because of the public's increased awareness of climate change, decentralized stormwater management now has great market potential. Which may explain why the hardware store did not balk at the expensive cost of TV air time.

Should a client, inspired by just such a TV commercial, decide to install rainwater recycling in their new garden, then at least in Switzerland, well-prepared brochures are readily available which offer informative diagrams of all the possibilities and options. However, after careful study, particularly when the precise dimensioning of the installation is to be decided upon, these brochures often prove difficult to understand and in practice are only of limited use to the non-expert. In addition, this complex topic requires carefully handling by public authorities, as it must be ensured that no hazardous substances infiltrate into and pollute the subsoil or groundwater. In small projects the budget is often too small to include the services of specialists, such as a hydro-geologist. Consequently, designers and contractors must be in a position to evaluate and implement rainwater retention and infiltration in small projects. The CTI (Swiss Innovation Promotion Agency) has sponsored one such project at the University of Applied Sciences Rapperswil. An Internet portal, ‹regenwassermanagement.ch›, has been developed; it offers support to garden and landscape contractors as well as offices designing and detailing stormwater management for small projects. The site's contents are based on the planning process, which is broken down into the following steps:

Basic Information
00. Fees and Charges
01. Priorities
02. Laws and Regulations
03. When Planning Permission is Required
04. When Planning Permission is Not Required

Microsoft Excel calculation programs and formulae are work aids included under the individual points. But what does stormwater management have to do with site grading?

During "optimization", site grading is the deciding tool that enables the infiltration of stormwater on site. Even just by raising the levels of paths and hardscape areas, the spaces that lie between can become green areas for infiltrating and retaining rainwater. Rainwater that falls on roofs should be collected from the gutters and downspouts and not put into a concrete pipe connected to the sewer system, but conveyed in open drainage chan-

Fig. 6.1 left: A park in Phoenix, Arizona, between a parking lot and two very busy streets. The grading, implemented at little cost and effort, transformed the space from a traffic island into a park.

Fig. 6.2 right: A shallow swale conveys the runoff from the parking lot to a sunken hollow in the middle. Here the water can infiltrate on site and consequently save money.

HSR / KTI Projekt
"Regenwassermanagement für den Schweizer GaLaBau"

ilf Institut für Landschaft und Freiraum

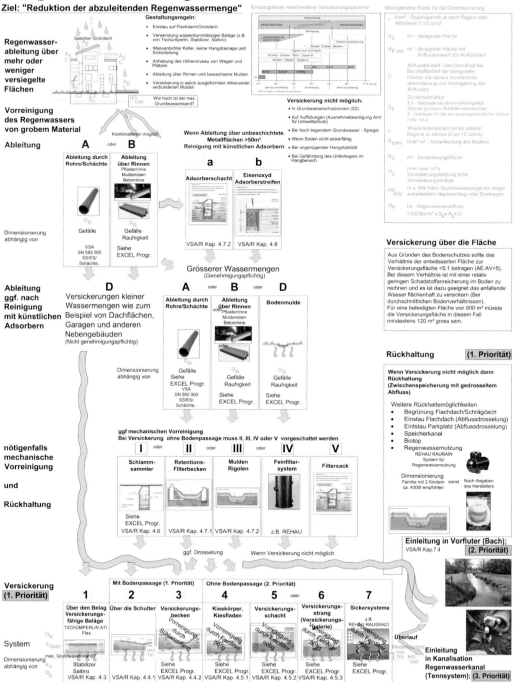

nels and allowed to flow into softly landscaped swales. Using swales and surface drainage channels, the elevations of which are determined during site grading, a simple and networked infiltration system can be created with very little effort. The landscape architect and stormwater management expert Michael Fluss speaks in this context of "communicating swales". This is an inexpensive system that needs little maintenance. Open drainage channels are much easier to clean and maintain than pipes. In addition "communicating swales" save on stormwater runoff fees. Large cities charge for stormwater runoff and use this charge as an incentive for on-site infiltration in order to take the pressure off the existing sewer systems. On-site infiltration is not only easy on the wallet but also on local ecology, as the rainwater takes the shortest route back to its natural rainwater circulation system.

The combination of green roofs, permeable paving and surface infiltration is most efficient. The ideal situation is as follows: rainwater is retained by green roofing, and is slowly released via the downspout to a rainwater cistern, from where it can be reused for garden irrigation. The excess water flows via open drain channels into swales, where it can infiltrate. Rainwater that falls on paved surfaces runs into adjacent planting areas. The edges of the planted areas enable the water to spread evenly amongst the planting and lawn surfaces and thus avoiding waterlogging.

Fig. 6.3 left: Stormwater management workflow chart.

Fig. 6.4 top: Rainwater storage cistern for garden irrigation.

Fig. 6.5 top: Rainwater runs from the downspout into an open swale.

Fig. 6.6 center: A rectangular section drainage channel with its own grade conveys any uninfiltrated rainwater to a second swale area.

Fig. 6.7 bottom: The second swale "communicates" with the first via the grading and the drainage channel and is able to take on extra quantities of rainwater.

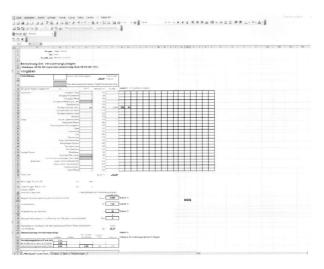

Fig. 6.8 top: An infiltration test determines the specific infiltration rate S, and is an integral procedure in rainwater management design.

Fig. 6.9 center: Excel tables with the specific S value entered help to dimension infiltration and retention installations.

Fig. 6.10 bottom left: The stormwater management concept is developed on the basis of the Excel calculations.

Fig. 6.11 bottom right: The garding plan, with spot elevations and slopes, is developed from the stormwater management concept.

When surface infiltration rates are low, a subsurface channel system can be constructed composed of subsurface channels filled with gravel. Thus, in addition to surface storage, the additional retention volume of the cavity spaces in the gravel is available. In spatially tight situations and sometimes for safety reasons (protection of small children when water levels rise above 20 centimeters) off-the-shelf system components can be installed underground, again retaining the rainwater and slowly allowing it to infiltrate.

These innovative systems for retaining stormwater are gaining an increasing share of the market. Underground retention system elements ideally come into play in situations where ponds, basins and swales cannot be implemented for spatial, design or safety reasons. These sponge-like units can now withstand the pressure of up to 3 meters of soil cover. The conveyed rainwater first runs through an initial sediment filter, and then a cleansing chamber to trap dissolved pollutants, thus substituting the cleaning effect of a living soil layer. The storage units are made from PE (polyethylene) and have a storage capacity of 95%; water can flow through them from many directions. They are an intermediate and buffer storage area that relieves pressure on the sewer system, are very flexible, and can be "hidden" underground. In the medium term, because of technical improvements in plastics, and because they are standardized and accepted by public authorities, these rainwater recycling and infiltration installations offer good value for money. Widespread use in residential, commercial and industrial sites is foreseeable. Thus, stormwater management becomes possible in projects where the argument "there is no space for stormwater on our site" was previously used.

Fig. 6.12 left: A retention system built several meters deep into the earth. However, health and safety requirements were not met during construction. Regulations stipulate that deep excavation walls be protected with temporary sheet piling.

Fig. 6.13 right: A single RAUSIKKO retention unit.

Fig. 6.14 top: A grass swale with subsurface retention elements.

Fig. 6.15 center: Swale with natural planting.

Fig. 6.16 bottom: A swale with garden flair.

Fig. 6.17 top: Rainwater run-off needs to be guaranteed even for large storm events. Paving manufacturers recommend a minimum fall of 3%, even when permeable paving is used. The underlying layers (bedding course, subbase, etc.) should have the same gradient as the paving surface.

Fig. 6.18 bottom: Stabilizer is a permeable paving surface, popular in Switzerland. It can be installed with a surface gradient of up to 17%. As with other compacted mineral surfaces, it requires a minimum gradient of 1.5%.

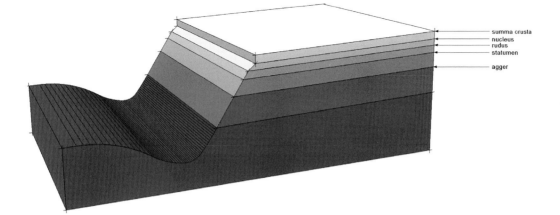

summa crusta
nucleus
rudus
statumen

agger

Fig. 6.19: Cross section through a Roman road. Even then, attention was paid to ensure that rainwater could run off the paving surface into ditches running along the sides (see Eidenbenz 2001, p. 8). This construction method still is suitable for road construction.

Fig. 6.20: U-drains, mud traps, inspection manholes and piping are not only part of normal property drainage but are also the basic building blocks of rainwater management.

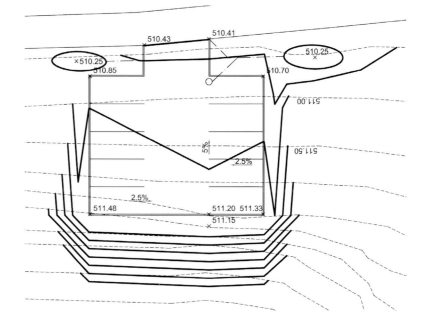

Site Grading and Stormwater Management Case Studies

Case Study 1: Stormwater runoff from of a parking lot, which has a 5% longitudinal gradient and 2.5% cross fall, runs from a paved open surface drain to a manhole and from there into the right-hand swale. The water from the remaining area where the parking lot meets the street is collected in a rectangular section drainage channel with a grate, and conveyed to the swale on the left. The permeable paving is edged with a curb at the same level as the paving. Shallow swales run around the parking lot collecting the runoff water from the surrounding embankments. This collected water infiltrates, together with the parking lot runoff, in the main swales to the left and right. The main swales are connected by a pipe. This helps balance the load in long rain events.

Case Study 2: The rainwater runoff from the roof of a building and its surrounding terrace are to be infiltrated on site. The areas around the house have a gradient of 2.5%. Limited by the hillside location, two swales convey the rainwater. The saddle point lies on the hill side of the house, outside of the surface area to be drained. It is deeper than the terrace but just a little higher than one of the contour lines (37.01). Using this trick, the contour lines run back before the spot level of the saddle, adding overall clarity to the contour plan. Both swales end in an infiltration hollow.

Case Study 3: A system of swales, connected by pipes and in the path areas by open surface drains, retains and infiltrates the rainwater that falls on the paved surfaces.

Fig. 6.21: Site grading and stormwater design of a parking lot.

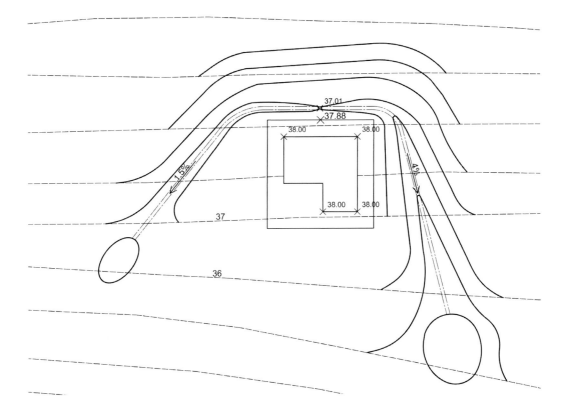

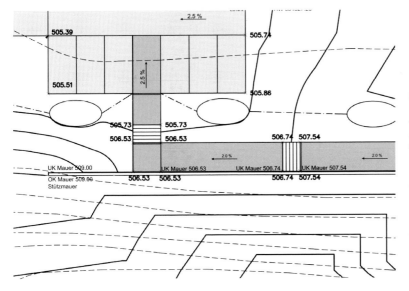

Fig. 6.22: The runoff from the roof flows to the swales via the roof gutters, downspouts, and paved surfaces. The swales have both cross and longitudinal gradient and provide space for the water to infiltrate.

Fig. 6.23: "Communicating swales" collect water from the paved surface, and convey the water to lower-lying swales during long rain events.

Digital Site Grading

Data from Local Survey Offices

Property boundaries, building and land use are legally defined in cadastral survey plans. For some sites, the brass survey markers with reference elevations can be found with the help of the cadastral plan. Further
elevation information can be generally obtained from the same public
authorities who normally administer the cadastral survey plans, in the
form of digital contour maps or as ASCII code. ASCII stands for "American
Standard Code for Information Interchange" and contains a maximum of
256 characters. The data can be opened with a simple text editor. Otherwise, the format DXF (drawing exchange format) developed by Autodesk
is a common exchange format for digital plans. Incidentally, DXF is also
an ASCII code.

Digital cadastral survey plans contain countrywide standardized coordinate values. Designers are often eager to shift the origin of their drawing to null (0,0,0) in CAD so that they can work with smaller coordinate
values. They also like to rotate the digital plan to produce a better layout.
However, when no reference point is defined, the site's location within the
national coordinate system is lost. Using national coordinates has several
important advantages over working with a shifted plan. Drawing without
theuse of the national coordinate system is strongly discouraged. The advantages are:
— All data, from architects, engineers and other professionals are
  aligned. Coordination mistakes, which can always happen when
  plans are being worked on, are much easier to identify.
— Elevations, the axes of walls, steps and paths, and the location of
  trees are explicitly defined using national coordinates. Their respec-
  tive easting and northing also serve as setting-out data for the construction site.

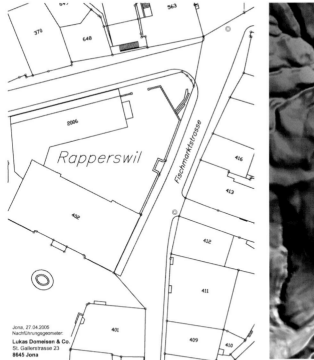

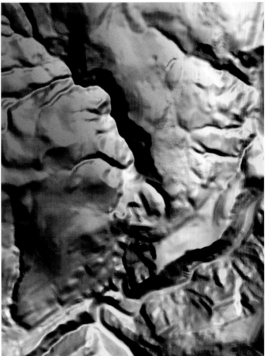

Jona, 27.04.2005
Nachführungsgeometer:
Lukas Domeisen & Co.
St. Gallerstrasse 23
8645 Jona

Fig. 7.1 top left: Excerpt from the cadastral survey map of Rapperswil-Jona.

Fig. 7.2 top center: Metal boundary marker from the official ordinance survey.

Fig. 7.3 top right: Tüfentobel landfill, matrix site model in Global Mapper.

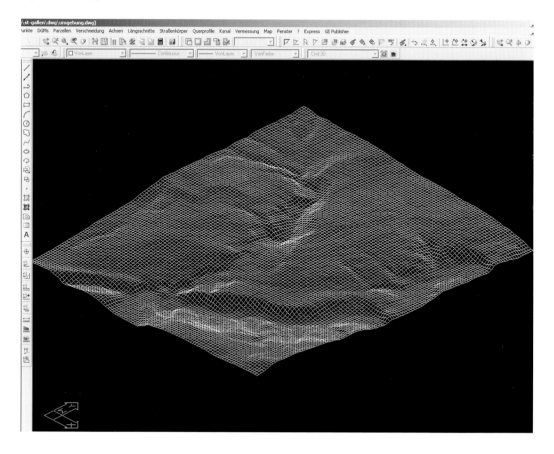

Care is needed when referring to x and y coordinates in surveying. CAD programs use the Cartesian coordinate system. The horizontal axis is termed the abscissa, x-axis or easting axis. The vertical axis is called the ordinate, y-axis or northing. In surveying, easting and northing define the location of elements, where y stands for easting and x for northing!

In large projects the responsible local authority may want to provide elevations in the form of grid data. The "Picture Cell Elements" (PIXEL) have a uniform size and are ordered in a matrix. Every computer user knows about pixels from the latest image processing programs. For elevation plans in grid format, each pixel has an additional attribute value for the site elevation. To be able to use this in a CAD program, either the supplier needs to convert the data into contour lines, or an inexpensive program such as Global Mapper (‹globalmapper.com›) should be used to convert the raster elevation data into vector-based elevation information.

Fig. 7.4: An elevation model imported from Global Mapper into Civil 3D.

Data Mapping with GPS

GPS is a system supported by a constellation of 24 satellites, which provides the user with relatively precise position data. The first widespread function of GPS receivers is for simple navigation. Instantaneous locationing is delivered with a margin of error around 30 to 50 meters. The receiver is small, easy to transport, and does not cost much. The latest mobile phones offer GPS technology.

Differential GPS (DGPS) uses a second, stationary GPS receiver to correct the measurements of the first. A stationary reference station (base station) and a mobile receiver (rover) are used. The reference station is equipped with radio communication and transmits the data it receives from the satellites. The rover is also equipped with a radio link and receives this information signal from the reference station, providing data directly from the satellites via the rover's GPS antenna. Thus, two data sets are received by the rover in real time, which means they can be immediately processed, giving a highly accurate location. Surveyors, in particular, use this differential GPS technology.

A less expensive alternative is equipment with the capacity to receive corrective data with the receiver and use them to increase the precision of the location. A further variation is to correct the collected data the next day using the Internet. This method is known as post-processing, where corrective GPS data are available online 24 hours after the data mapping. Using this corrective information, the data collected the day before can be adjusted. Measurements taken with a GPS receiver, mobile phone or the post-processing method are suitable for data collection in the open landscape (for mapping). When site boundaries are being determined, accuracy to within centimeters is required. Elevation is more problematic, as the typical level of accuracy is limited to meters.

Fig. 7.5 above left: Collecting data with a GPS GS20 from Leica Geosystems.

Fig. 7.6 above right: GPS with an antenna provides better reception.

Fig. 7.7 below left: Ease of use is the great advantage of the new generation of tacheometers, for example the Builder R100/200M from Leica Geosystems.

Fig. 7.8 below right: The Builder is put to use at the University of Applied Sciences Rapperswil.

Data Collection Using a Builder's Tacheometer

"A surveyor's level (or dumpy level, builder's level or automatic level) is a measuring instrument with which differences in levels can be measured and horizontal levels can be set."

"The theodolite [...] is an angle measurement instrument. It is used in geodetics (the science of surveying) to measure horizon directions and zenith and vertical angle." (Wikipedia: http://de.wikipedia.org, 9.12.2007).

The tacheometer is a further evolution of the theodolite and can be used to measure distance in addition to measuring angles.

GPS is much discussed and used. It is a technology which is now frequently used for landscape architecture mapping projects. But is GPS always the right solution? When taking levels on construction sites, where there may, for example, be reception shadows (i.e. no reception from the GPS satellites), a tacheometer is a much better option. Offices and companies who decide to purchase a tacheometer give the following reasons:

— A proper survey company is too expensive for small survey tasks.
— Bought plans are often incomplete or do not include the desired information about the site. For example, planting areas, tree crown diameters, and decorative elements are often missing, or there is too little detail.
— The designers can take targeted measurements to assist the design of important changes in level such as walls, steps etc.
— Quantity survey plans are very time-intensive. This work can be made more effective by combining tacheometer and CAD.
— The simple menu structure makes it easy to learn how to use the tacheometer.
— Setting up the equipment, defining the instrument location, and working with a self-defined construction axis are uncomplicated. To map information based on national coordinates, a setting-out axis consisting of two points and one elevation point must be known.
— When the surveying is finished, the transmission of ASCII data can occur via a USB cable. Staking out data, prepared in the office with CAD, can also be transmitted to the tacheometer without a problem.

Digital Site Grading

Fig. 7.9 left: ASCII data in a text editor.

Fig. 7.10 right: The same ASCII data in Civil 3D.

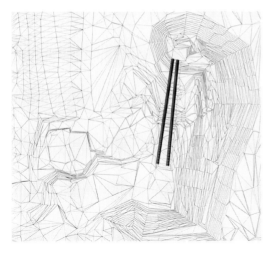

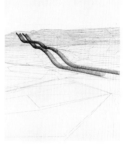

Digital Models

A triangulated irregular network (TIN) is a digital data structure form used to represent a terrain surface. The TIN data structure is based on two elements: points and edges. Triangulation tessellates the data using triangles to form a surface. The more points and edges in a model, the more varied the possibilities for triangulation are. Long, narrow triangles can cause inaccuracy. Delaunay triangulation limits the occurrence of these awkward shapes. For example, when the civil engineering program Civil 3D (from Autodesk) uses ASCII data and the Delaunay triangulation method to calculated the TIN, it intermeshes the points so effectively that no other points are to be found within the circle created by the three points of any given triangle.

TIN are created not just from points but also from breaklines. What are breaklines? Retaining walls, which impede the collapse of a steep hillside, are a classical example of a breakline. The top and bottom edge of dam embankments are also breaklines. These can greatly affect the triangulation of a model.

In plan, the top edge of a vertical retaining wall lies directly over the bottom edge. The TIN algorithms do not allow the triangulation of points or lines that lie directly on top of one another. Experienced 3D digital modelers circumvent this problem by constructed two lines parallel and very close to one another. The first line is the bottom edge, and the second

Fig. 7.11 left: TIN of the project Ravensburg Playland Phase III. Design: Rotzler Krebs Partner Landscape Architects BSLA, digital terrain model: Peter Petschek.

Fig. 7.12 right: Rendered site model, Ravensburg Playland Phase III.

Fig. 7.13 below right: A slide integrated into the digital site model, Ravensburg Playland Phase III.

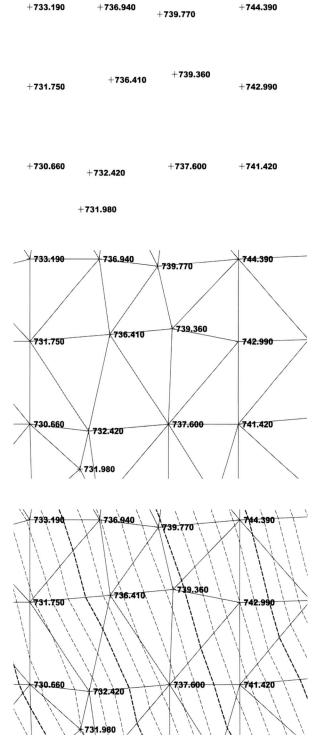

+733.190   +736.940
                    +739.770   +744.390

                    +739.360
            +736.410
+731.750   +742.990

+730.660   +737.600   +741.420
        +732.420

    +731.980

Fig. 7.14 top: Spot elevations for a site data set.

Fig. 7.15 center: TIN of the elevation data.

Fig. 7.16 bottom: Representation of the TIN as a contour plan with 1 m intervals.

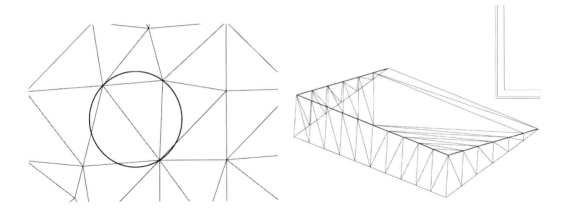

the top edge. The program is able to triangulate these lines easily. That is why in effect walls are always constructed as if tapered in digital elevation models. Tunnels and overhangs are an even greater challenge. They can only be constructed with the help of circumventions. Using the TIN surfaces as a basis, it is easy to identify the elevation of any given point as well as the slope of a given area. In addition, contour lines can be automatically produced using TIN.

One problem in the construction of a TIN based on imported or drawn contour lines is the occurrence of level triangles. Each triangle should actually connect higher and lower lying points. As there may sometimes be no appropriate level on a higher line nearby, the program triangulates with the next-nearest point on the same contour line. A level area is created where there is actually a slope. This error causes mistakes in quantity estimations. Professional digital modeling programs have commands to rotate triangles.

The generation of a digital terrain model is mostly automatic. The origin of the input data can vary widely, starting with data collected oneself with a tacheometer to contour lines digitalized manually, to commercially obtained survey data. It should be explicitly emphasized that the precision of the model and calculations depend on the quality of the input data. Visual verification of the digital model by someone with knowledge of the site is always recommended.

Fig. 7.17 left: Using Delaunay triangulation, no other point is found within the circle defined by the points of any arbitrary triangle. This helps reduce inaccuracies.

Fig. 7.18 right: A retaining wall as isometric and plan in detail. The outer line in the plan is the wall's bottom edge, both inner lines are the top edge.

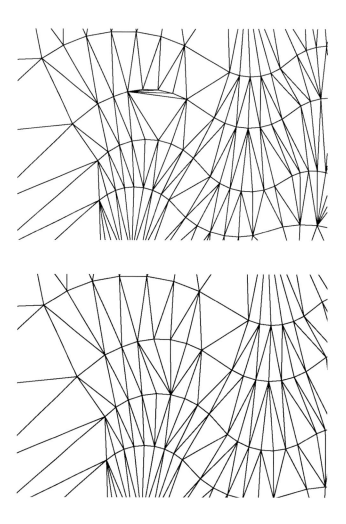

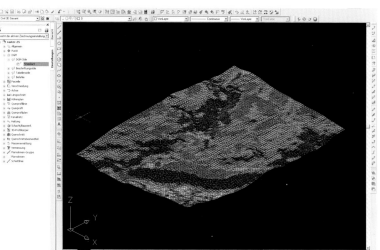

Fig. 7.19 top: Faulty TIN – several triangles tessellate with the same contour line.

Fig. 7.20 center: Correct TIN-triangles tessellate between higher and lower contour lines.

Fig. 7.21 bottom: Elevation analysis using a digital terrain model.

Site Model Making

History

Between 1762 and 1786, Franz Ludwig Pfyffer built a scale model entitled "Relief of Primordial Switzerland". This was the first three-dimensional landscape model that topographically represented a spezific area.
The alpine region around Lucerne with Lake Lucerne and the neighboring
Cantons is replicated at a scale of 1:12,500, with light vertical exaggeration
and great detail. Shortly after its completion, the 26 m^2 model became a
popular attraction in Lucerne. Discerning travelers such as Johann Wolf-
gang von Goethe were delighted to be able to look at the mountains from
above. Hot air balloons and alpine tourism were still unknown at this time.
One can imagine the fascination that this model landscape exerted on
viewers: until then, the landscape had only been seen from the perspective of a foot traveler, or from a carriage. And as such, only as segments,
which were often rather threatening or tiresome to the traveler. Pieces of
wood, coal, brick, plaster and sand, covered with a painted layer of bees-
wax were the materials used to create this first landscape model.

Digital Model Making

Today, specialist computer programs and plotters have taken over the
role of making landscape models, naturally using digital models as input data. Contour lines must be closed and each have its own layer for
a specialist CAD/CAM system to be able to import DXF or DWG format

Fig. 7.22: "Relief of Primordial Switzerland" was
finished by Franz Ludwig
Pfyffer in 1786, and is found
today in the Gletschergarten
Lucerne.

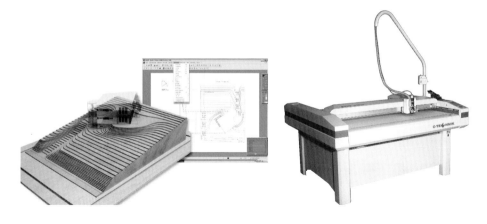

files. Once the data have been processed by an architectural model-making program, a toolhead cutting plotter shapes the model using either an automatically controlled cutting blade for cork or cardboard, or a routing head for plastic or wood. Alternative techniques are milling down or constructing layers. In the former, automatic cutting robots mill the relief from a block. In the latter, a 3D plotter uses fluid plastic to construct the terrain, layer by layer. Both of these methods are only suitable for small models.

Analog Sand Model

Did you play with wet sand on the beach during your last holiday? Sandcastles are much loved. A small tip for ambitious sandcastle builders: Google the words "sandcastle competition"; you will be amazed to find there is even a sandcastle world cup.

Moist sand is the best building material for site models. It is a very good analog alternative to cardboard layer models, as the site can be presented as smooth. With cardboard layer models, the terraces can sometimes be distracting, depending on the thickness of the card. There are also products available which simulate sand using a wax additive. The benefits compared to natural sand is that they never dry out. And if you want, the model can even be baked in the oven! The best place to ask is in a toyshop.

Building a sand model is child's play. The problems with this technique start with the transfer of information. Landscape architects and architects want to get their ideas built. Plans, earthwork calculations, and costing are needed. How do you translate a sand model into a drawing? The tradition-

Fig. 7.23 left: Architectural and site model created using CAMOD software from C-Technik and a Zünd flatbed cutter.

Fig. 7.24 right: Zünd flatbed cutter with a router toolhead.

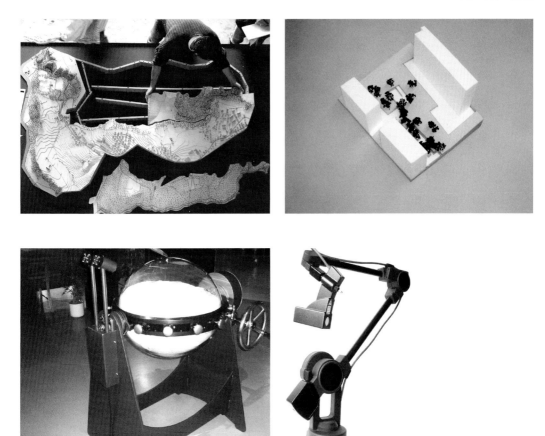

al method is to construct a grid over the model and measure the distance to the model at each grid point. This method is reminiscent of how contour maps were drawn 300 years ago, and to get straight to the point: too much effort, too inaccurate and too unprofessional.

3D Laser Scanner

A more futuristic solution is to use a 3D laser scanner. This is a machine that uses laser beams to read a three-dimensional shape and prepares a digital model from the accumulated data. This technique is also known as "reverse engineering". It provides the digital compilation of drawing-less objects as "point clouds", which allow it to be further developed in 3D CAD.

Fig. 7.25 top left: Tüfentobel Landfill, St. Gallen – the elevation model in 2 mm grey card was made using a flatbed cutter.

Fig. 7.26 top right: Landscape model using Deltasand, sand with added wax.

Fig. 7.27 bottom left: The exhibit "Sand Landscapes" at Technorama – the Swiss Science Center in Winterthur shows how landscapes form and erode. Visitors can use the crank levers to influence how formations occur in the sand model.

Fig. 7.28 bottom right: A laser sensor mounted onto the reader head of a digitalizer scans complex three-dimensional shapes.

Echtzeitmodell Deponie Tüfentobel
Hochschule für Technik Rapperswil, Landschaftsarchitektur, August 2007.

Kamera Maussteuerung (fliegen)
Maustasten: links - vorwärts | rechts - zurück
Pfeiltasten: links/rechts - Pan
Bild auf/ab: Höhenänderung rauf/runter
Leertaste: Kamera zurücksetzen

Kamera-Varianten um die Varianten zu aktivieren, drücken Sie
Ausbau-Varianten

K   Kamera Maussteuerung
     Kamera Bodennähe

A   S   D   F   G   H
Bestand Etappe 1 Etappe 2 Etappe 3 Etappe 4 Endzustand

Entsorgungsamt

Amt für Umweltschutz (AFU)
Baudepartement
des Kantons St.Gallen

Real-time Models

"Well, how about that! The site looks totally different in the plans and model." This exclamation is often heard on construction projects. The world of plans and models all too often only includes professionals. Drawings contain abbreviations and symbols that a layperson does not understand. Sand, plaster, card and wood models require a high level of imagination to understand them. A design can only be successful when all those involved and the future users understand and support it. In short, when the kids at home are using their game consoles to navigate through the world's best 3D graphics, the architect putting a drawing and abstract model on the table is no longer able to convince the parents, nor is the urban planner's black and white overhead on the wall enough at the local council meeting to get people to understand the proposed project. A research project revealed that our seeing habits, amongst other reasons conditioned by the omnipresent games industry, move increasingly in interactive patterns. In a questionnaire regarding the computer animation of a park proposal,

Fig. 7.29 left: A real-time model of the Tüfentobel landfill, St. Gallen, using Workflow Civil 3D – Autodesk VIZ – Quest 3D.

the researchers made the following observations: "Noticeably many of those asked were able to recommend possible improvements. Above all, they wanted interaction. They desired individual route selection, choice of perspective, choice of location, and the ability to reverse." (Petschek / Lange 2003, p.14).

In contrast to animations, real-time models have the advantage that one can move about interactively in them. High-tech graphic cards are now included as standard in PCs, which enables the use of real-time 3D visualization. With the help of these graphic cards, calculations can be performed in real time, i.e. more than 25 images per second. All modern 3D computer games are based on this technology, and programs such as Autodesk VIZ can export terrain models as real-time environments easily. Google Earth™ map services are a good base for the presentation of 3D site models. Autodesk's Civil 3D supports direct exportation into the Internet environment.

Fig. 7.30 top left: Playful use of a real-time model in a citizen-friendly exhibit of an urban design project in Barcelona.

Fig. 7.31 top right: The easy-to-understand presentation of a landscape architectural competition using a touch screen.

Fig. 7.32 bottom: Real-time model of the Michaelsberg Monastery in Bamberg by Schildwächter Ingenieure, planning for real and virtual space, Hochspeyer / Kaisers-lautern, 2007.

Landscape Stabilization

Two terms define sloped landscape elements:
— Hill
— Embankment

While hill describes a natural landform, embankment refers to an artificial earthwork structure. There is no particular reason for this differentiation in terms of structural stability. Regardless of whether it is in a hill or an embankment, soil will slip or collapse when the incline of the slopes exceeds the shearing resistance of the soil material. Landslides and soil erosion can cause devastating catastrophes. The following pages give an overview of soil stabilization construction techniques used to prevent soil slips and erosion.

Soil

Geotechnology differentiates between unconsolidated rock and bedrock. Bedrock includes a range from granite to *nagelfluh* (conglomerate), where the microstructure is durably bonded by minerals. Unconsolidated rock can be subdivided according to particle size. The following particle diameters define six mineral size classes:
— Clay   < 0.002 mm
— Silt   0.002 – 0.06 mm
— Sand   0.06 – 2.0 mm
— Gravel   2.0 – 6.0 mm
— Cobble   6.0 – 200 mm
— Boulder   > 200 mm

A particle distribution curve indicates the sum total of a sieved material shown as particle size distribution. Using these measurements and other criteria, a given soil can be classified into a soil class with same or similar characteristics. The loadbearing capacity, workability and frost and water capacity of soils can be estimated based on the soil class.

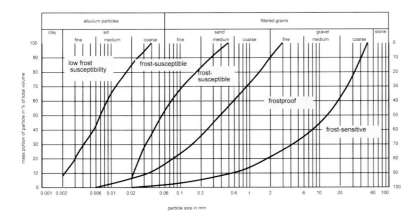

In practice, geotechnical laboratories carry out testing and give on-site recommendations on the workability and stability of the soil.

Naturally occurring soil "grows" over thousands of years, forming soil horizons of A topsoil, B subsoil and C substratum. The substratum is composed of either unconsolidated or consolidated rock without soil accumulation or the presence of biological activity. The transitional layer is of weathered base material which is usually well interspersed with roots. This is the subsoil and extends to depths of 50–150 centimeters. The topsoil layer is organically active, rich in humus, darkly colored, and usually has extensive root development. The topsoil is normally between 5 and 40 centimeters thick.

Soil that is to be excavated, transported, distributed, and driven on should be treated as follows:
— Soil should be excavated and deposited only if the soil water tension level equals ≥ 10 cbar. Soil water tension is the energy needed to hold back the water in the soil pores and surfaces. The drier the soil, the greater its water tension is. This measurement is of central importance during earthworks because of the soil's loadbearing capacity and degree of dampness. Soil water tension is measured with a tensiometer. The measurement unit is the centibar (cbar/cb).
 - 0 to 6 cbar = wet soil
 - 6 to 12 cbar = damp soil
 -12 to 20 cbar = damp to drying soil
 - > 20 cbar = dry soil, ideal to be worked.
 Practitioners recommend not walking on, driving on, or working the soil when it is kneadable (plastic).
— Wheeled vehicles should be used only on the substratum or on defined circulation tracks.

Fig. 8.1: Particle size distribution chart showing frost-proof and frost-susceptible soils.

— Drainage must be provided for while the earthworks are being carried out.
— The difference in pH value between the topsoil and subsoil may not exceed 0.7 pH units. Using soils with greatly differing degrees of acidity results in very different soil solution environments, and may restrict plant and root growth.
— Soil should be laid in layers of maximum 0.5 meters and each layer should be compacted (FaBo, 2003).

For the interim storage of soil:
— Drainage must be provided for.
— No other materials should be stored at the interim soil storage area.
— The soil should not be driven over. The soil should be loosely piled up and immediately planted with vegetation.
— The maximum height for stockpiling topsoil is ≤ 2.5 meters for interim storage of less than one year and ≤ 1.5 meters for storage lasting longer than one year.
— The maximum height for stockpiling subsoil varies from ≤ 1.5 meters for delicate soils to > 2.5 meters for more robust soils.
— Topsoil and subsoil should be excavated separately and stored separately.
— Mixing clean soil with polluted soil should be avoided (FaBo, 2003).

Fig. 8.2: Sieving tower used to determine soil particle size distribution.

Excavating soil changes its volume. For topsoil, an expansion factor of 1.2 is used for the transition from a dense to a loose state. The expansion

factor for subsoil and substratum is approximately 1.3.

When topsoil has been redistributed it will settle and compact naturally, its volume changing by a factor of 0.85. Newly laid subsoil and substratum have a settling factor of 0.75. Clean sand and other frostproof materials used for the base course have the following expansion and settling factors: solid – loose 1.25 and loose – solid 0.8.

Erosion and Landslides

Erosion

Erosion and landslides are the two main dangers in site grading. The Romans used the term *erodere* for "erode". Hence the English word "rodent". In Italian, the word "erodere" today means "wash out". In contrast to soil erosion, erosion is the natural weathering process of rock on the surface of the earth. Soil erosion means the movement and transfer of soil caused by humans. Water erosion and mechanical erosion are two additional types of erosion.

Plowing and the compaction of a site through hikers or grazing animals cause mechanical changes. In steep meadows in the Alps, animals tend to walk in tracks parallel to the slopes. These animal tracks are an example of mechanical soil erosion; soil researchers call them track slips *(Trittblaiken)*.

Fig. 8.3: A tensiometer used for measuring soil water tension (‹ums-muc.de›).

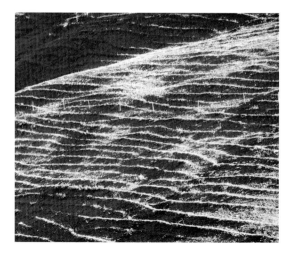

Fig. 8.4 top: These animal tracks in the Tössbergen are an example of mechanical erosion, the product of animal grazing.

Fig. 8.5 center: Even excavation sites sometimes look like art. The plastic wrapping is for protection against water erosion.

Fig. 8.6 bottom: Sand dunes: a product of wind erosion.

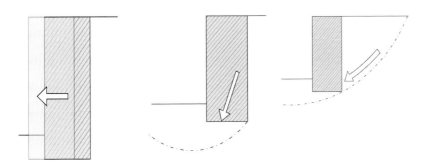

Water erosion is triggered by heavy and extended rain events. A closed vegetation layer restricts water erosion. On a construction site, plastic sheeting does the job of protecting excavations from water.

Fine, sandy soils are particularly susceptible to wind erosion; sand dunes are one result. Wind breaks such as natural stone walls or plantings are used in many countries to protect against wind erosion.

Landslides

The earth's gravity is the cause of landslides, for as soon as its shearing resistance is too small, soil moves downwards. "Landslide" is used in geotechnology as an umbrella term for damage caused by soil breaches. Geotechnical scientists differentiate the downhill movement of soil into the different categories of topsoil landslides, translational slips, slumps and shear failure. Common causes of landslides are:
— Infiltration of surface water
— Very steep inclines
— Excavation at the embankment foot
— Tremors, earthquakes
— Too much weight on the crown of the embankment or earth structure

Suitable countermeasures should be coordinated with a geotechnical engineer. Careful attention should be paid to the foundation soil on a construction site. Every large site-grading project should start with a geotechnical survey.

Fig. 8.7: A failing wall in the form of a translational slide, rotational slide, and a slump (from left to right).

Embankment Angle and Construction Technology

Depending on the embankment's angle of slope, the following constructive methods are suitable for stabilizing embankments and hillsides:

0° to 33.7°

Stabilization measures are not necessary at this relatively low range of steepness. However, even the flattest slope needs to be vegetated. The standard slope of normal soil type embankments in road construction is around 33.7° (2:3). Temporary erosion protection is recommended (using, for example, a natural textile) to get vegetation established as soon as possible.

33.7° to 45°

An incline angle between 33.7° (2:3) and 45° (1:1) requires soil stabilization. Bioengineering construction methods or soil reinforcement with surface protection are suitable.

45° to 70°

An embankment angle greater than 45° is referred to as "oversteep". Reinforced earth, geotextile walls and to a certain extent bioengineering construction techniques are appropriate stabilization methods.

70° to 90°

Fig. 8.8: Embankment stabilization works on a bypass, Canton Zurich.

Only a retaining wall can stabilize a slope with an angle of incline between 70° and 90°.

An Overview of Slope Stabilization Construction Techniques

This section gives an overview of the various stabilization techniques that can be employed to reduce erosion and landslides in site grading. The author urgently reminds the reader that the following construction techniques should only be used in consultation with professional experts.

— Bioengineering construction methods (soil protection and ground stabilization methods)
— Lime and cement stabilization
— Reinforced earth
— Geotextiles
— Retaining walls (gravity and cantilever)

Bioengineering Construction Methods

Bioengineering combines technical and biological knowledge. Plants take center stage. Plant roots not only take up nutrients; their root systems also stabilize the soil. Some plants reproduce asexually. Cuttings are planted, and by the next spring leaves uncurl on the thin saplins and new roots have already anchored into the soil. In this special area of landscape architecture, plants have not only an aesthetic and ecological function but serve primarily as a construction material to conserve soil. In this context we refer to live implementation. Construction methods that use living material are complex and depend heavily on local habitat factors such as soil, water, climate and the availability of local vegetation. Numerous publications deal with this topic skillfully and in depth. This section of the book is simply a brief introduction to the topic. If bioengineering construction methods are to be employed, study of technical literature (e.g. Zeh 2007)

Fig. 8.9: Embankment stabilization using coconut netting, Leutschenbach in Zurich (dipol Landschaftsarchitekten).

and consultation with local professionals are an absolute must if the project is to be implemented successfully.

Bioengineering applies soil protection methods to protect against soil erosion and ground stabilizing techniques to prevent landslides.

Soil Protection Techniques

Soil protection techniques protect the top soil layer from erosion. They include:

— Live brush mats. Branches are laid down closely packed with their thicker end pointing into the ground so that they can sprout. They are also secured with wooden stakes and wire, and then covered with earth.

— Erosion protection mats and nets. Erosion protection mats are usually seed mats constructed of two layers with the seed fixed between. Once the mats have been spread out over the embankment surface, stakes or pegs are used to anchor the mats to the ground. This same fixing method is used for nets. Biodegradable geotextile netting products cover the embankment and protect seeding from being washed away.

— Seeding. The simplest embankment stabilization is seeded turf or grass. The ideal sowing period extends from the beginning of April to mid-June and from the beginning of September to mid-October. Installing turf mats or rolls is expensive, but very effective.

— Wet seeding/hydroseeding. A mixture of glue, straw and seed is a typical surface treatment method used to vegetate road embankments. A mixing tank mounted on a truck is filled with environmentally friendly glue, meadow or shrub seeds, fertilizer, soil improvement compost, and water. The mixture is sprayed onto the embankment

Fig. 8.10: Construction of a willow live brush mat on the river Birs, designed by the landscape architecture office Geitz & Partner.

using a water cannon. In step two, the embankment is "shot" with straw. Mounted on the back of a truck, a large pneumatic pipe blows straw onto the artificial bank . Step three is to spread an additional layer of glue onto the straw to secure it to the ground.

Ground Stabilization Techniques

The purpose of ground stabilization construction methods is to prevent landslides. The methods are complex and are used only by specialist planners working together with specially equipped landscape contractors, who are able to carry out the construction procedures in extreme locations such as in the mountains or on hydraulic engineering projects. Ground stabilization methods include: layering, wattle fences, fascines and wooden stake fences.

In layering, there is a difference between brush layering, hedge layering and a combination of the two. The construction materials in brush layering are branches that are capable of sprouting, whereas rooting shrubs are used for hedge layering. The plant material is planted in stepped trenches, where the earth material of the upper trench is used to backfill the trench below, including the plant layering material. About 10 centimeters of the plant material is visible once the trench has been backfilled.

Bendy willow lengths or other sprouting rods are used to make the wattle fencing, which is secured with wooden stakes. Rods are also used to build fascines: bundles of long rods are laid in trenches, secured with wooden stakes and then covered up with earth. This construction technique originates in Italy and has been used in hydraulic engineering projects for hundreds of years. As an aside, in ancient Roman times the fasces were a bundle of rods with an axe, which officials carried in order to make way for important dignitaries. The term fascism finds its origin here too.

Fig. 8.11 left: To build a wooden stake fence, a structural frame of trunk sections is used in addition to sprouting branches to stabilize the embankment. A restoration project designed by the landscape architecture office Geitz & Partner.

Fig. 8.12 right: The completed project.

Fig. 8.13 top: Step 1: Spraying on the seed mixture.

Fig. 8.14 center: Step 2: Shooting on the straw.

Fig. 8.15 bottom: Step 3: Anchoring the straw with glue.

Lime and Cement Stabilization

Using lime and cement to stabilize the ground is not new in road and earthworks. The Romans mixed puzzolanic material into their roads. Pozzuoli is a small town at the foot of Mount Vesuvius, where volcanic ash has been mined since ancient times. The ash has characteristics similar to cement and was used in the production of concrete (Latin: opus caementitium).

A gravel and sand aggregate is the ideal material for road foundations. However, massive amounts are needed. Gravel and sand aggregates have the important ecological function of acting as a storage medium for ground water. As good aggregate becomes increasingly expensive and as the transportation of large quantities is harmful to the environment, lime and cement are increasingly being used to stabilize soils that are naturally unstable.

Soil stabilization enables the use of cohesive (binding) and wet soils. The addition of lime has an immediate effect on soil structure. In the long term, the hydrological and frost stability of the soil improves. Lime is used to stabilize clay soils, whereas cement is used to stabilize gravelly-sandy soils. A combination of lime and cement additives is appropriate for silt or silty sand.

Personnel who come into contact with unslaked lime during the on site mixing and installation procedures must wear protective clothing. In particular, the mouth and eyes must be protected. As a consequence, only contractors with specialist equipment use this technique. Lime stabilization is also sometimes used to waterproof pond bottoms and embankments.

Fig. 8.16: Ivy covered embankment, Baha'i Terraces and Gardens of Haifa, Israel.

Fig. 8.17: Embankment maintenance, Gardens of Haifa, Israel.

The BMX-Club "Grab on Kids" in Volketswil near Zurich wanted a new racing track. ARGE KIBAG/Innauen + Koch built the project in the spring of 2005. About 12,000 m³ of excavation material was used for the subgrade earthworks of the obstacle course, which was 380 m long and was between 5.5 and 10 m wide.

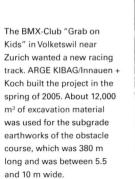

Fig. 8.18 top: The excavation material was graded into rough mounds by a 30 t excavator. After lime stabilization and compaction, smaller diggers were used to shape the professional standard race track.

Fig. 8.19 center: The surface material is crushed stone fines of 0–3 mm. The fines were mixed with water and applied like dough, then compacted using a vibrating plate.

Fig. 8.20 bottom: A test run.

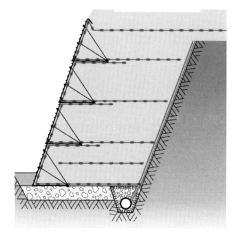

Reinforced Earth

Combined together, metal reinforcing mesh, geogrids, and fill material are known as "reinforced earth", "mechanically stabilized earth structures" or "terre armée". In addition to being financially interesting compared to concrete constructions, reinforced earth constructions also have the following advantages:

— High loadbearing capacity
— Not susceptible to subsidence
— Quick installation (60 m² per day is normal)
— Earthquake resistant
— Existing excavation material can generally be used
— There is no limit to the maximum built height

SYTEC TerraMur is a popular reinforced earth system in Switzerland. The galvanized or non-galvanized reinforcing meshes are inclined between 60° and 70°. Brackets ensure that the angle of inclination is maintained. Geogrids are synthetic mats and are fixed mechanically to the steel reinforcing. Once the geogrid has been laid out and covered with backfill, it is then folded up. The anchoring of the fill material in the webbing of the synthetic mats distributes tensile stress while acting as erosion protection for the front edge. There is a difference between front and backfill. Front material should be excavated earth without coarse granules and without organic material. A gravel and sand aggregate is the most suitable backfill material. Drainage behind the stabilizing reinforcement is indispensable.

Fig. 8.21: SYTEC TerraMur with the folded-up geogrid as mechanical stabilization. The side of the existing embankment must always be provided with drainage.

Fig. 8.22 top: TerraMur with TerraGreen vegetation.

Fig. 8.23 bottom: TerraMur after half a year planted with a low-maintenance extensive grass mixture.

Geotextile Retaining Walls

Geosynthetics are made from a polymer-based material. They come in various forms such as geotextiles, geonets and geogrids. Commonly used in geotechnology, these products have special functions, for example: separation, filtration, drainage, reinforcement, protection, waterproofing and erosion protection (Rüegger/Hufenus 2003). There are also biological-ly degradable geotextiles made from raw materials such as coconut, flax, cotton and jute. Natural-fiber slope stabilization materials remain func-tional for about one year, which is the normal time needed for roots to become established. Geosynthetic textiles last for more than ten years.

Geotextile retaining walls work on the same principle as reinforced earth. With the folding up of the geotextile sheet on the outer front, the geotextile wall looks like long, multi-layered piece of upholstery. Hence the synonym "geotextile barrel". The geotextile takes on the reinforcement function of the earth structure. The surface of the geotextile retaining wall must be vegetated, using either spray seeding or lines of shrubs. Depend-ing on the fill material, angles of incline up to 60° are possible.

Fig. 8.24 top: To stabilize an embankment, geotextile retaining walls made from stacked layers can also be built using natural fibers (coconut). A project by the landscape architecture office Geitz & Partner.

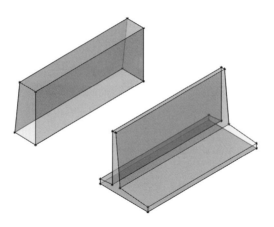

Retaining Walls

Fundamentally retaining walls are divided into cantilever retaining walls and gravity retaining walls. Both wall types need frostproof foundations or they will not be stable, because of frost heave and thaw settling. The accumulation of ice expands the soil and causes heave. During the subsequent thaw periods, the water content of the soil will change. This can result in uneven settling. In the lowlands in Switzerland, frost depth descends to 80 centimeters. High mountain areas more than 1500 meters above sea level have a frost depth of up to 250 centimeters.

Cantilever Retaining Walls

Cantilever walls are slim and suitable for large changes in elevation. The earth under the cantilever foot gives the wall stability. However, this stability depends on a wide cantilever foot on the embankment side and a lot of earth movement in comparison with a gravity wall. The wall should always be reinforced: the wall may be slim with very low concrete mass, but it must be high-strength. Cantilever retaining walls can be built vertically or with a backwards lean towards the embankment. The base and foot of the wall should have a slope of 10% to allow water to drain away from the substructure.

Fig. 8.25: A gravity wall is stable through its own weight. With a cantilever wall, the counterweight of the earth on the foundation foot makes it stable.

Fig. 8.26 right: Calculation of the foundation foot width of a cantilever retaining wall (Baukader Schweiz 2006, pp. 198–201).

Gravity Retaining Walls

The classic concrete gravity retaining wall has little or no reinforcement. The strength of the concrete is low, as are the width of the foundations, and the amount of excavation required. The large quantity of concrete required should be mentioned as a disadvantage. Gravity retaining

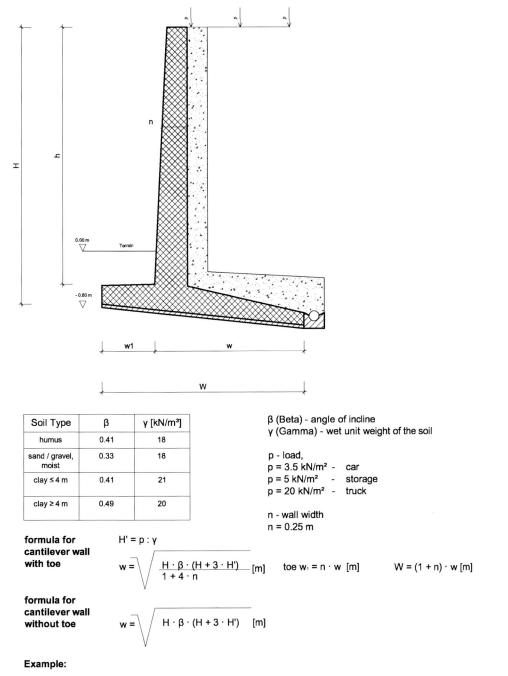

Soil Type	β	γ [kN/m³]
humus	0.41	18
sand / gravel, moist	0.33	18
clay ≤ 4 m	0.41	21
clay ≥ 4 m	0.49	20

β (Beta) - angle of incline
γ (Gamma) - wet unit weight of the soil

p - load,
p = 3.5 kN/m² - car
p = 5 kN/m²   - storage
p = 20 kN/m² - truck

n - wall width
n = 0.25 m

formula for cantilever wall with toe

$H' = p : \gamma$

$$w = \sqrt{\frac{H \cdot \beta \cdot (H + 3 \cdot H')}{1 + 4 \cdot n}} \ [m] \qquad \text{toe } w_1 = n \cdot w \ [m] \qquad W = (1 + n) \cdot w \ [m]$$

formula for cantilever wall without toe

$$w = \sqrt{H \cdot \beta \cdot (H + 3 \cdot H')} \ [m]$$

Example:

clay soil, wall height H = 3.0 m, P = 5 kN/m², cantilever wall with toe

$$H' = 5 : 21 = 0.24 \ m \qquad w = \sqrt{\frac{3.0 \cdot 0.41 \cdot (3.0 + 3 \cdot 0.24)}{1 + 4 \cdot 0.25}} = 1.51 \ m \qquad \text{toe } w_1 = 0.25 \times 1.51 = 0.38 \ m \qquad W = 1.89 \ m$$

Fig. 8.27: Gravity walls.

walls are suitable for good loadbearing soils and have a tapered incline of between 5:1 and 10:1. As a rule, the width of the foundations B is 40 to 50% of the height H, even in level sites. The category of gravity retaining walls includes: gabions, stone block walls, pre-cast element walls, and natural stone walls.

Gabions

"Gabbia" is Italian and means "cage", and actually gabions are related to wire cages. They have been used for over one hundred years to build gravity walls. They are stable, durable, resistant to settling and permeable. The relatively thin wire allows for quick constructive adjustments.

Similar to dry stone walls, the loose stone filling allows small organisms and plants to establish themselves within the gabion walls. The diversity of possible fill materials and even the integration of lighting are some of the reasons why gabions have found a place in garden design as an aesthetically pleasing retaining wall alternative.

Currently, gabions can be used for retaining walls up to a height of 3 meters. Why can bigger retaining elements not be used? The reason is structural. Gabion retaining walls are engineered as normal gravity walls. The principle is simple: the higher the wall, the wider the base. Using enormous amounts of stone is only economic if the stone can be found on site or nearby. As this is generally not the case, the height of a gabion wall is restricted.

Gabion walls require foundations, ideally made from a gravel and sand aggregate mixture. As with all retaining structures, attention must be paid to drainage. As gabions are permeable, it is sufficient to separate the gabions from the soil using a filter membrane. Geomembranes tend to become blocked, so you should use a filter membrane! Conventional

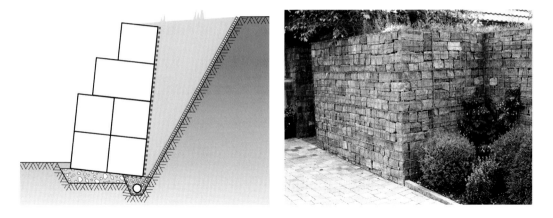

drainage using a combination of a drainage layer (for example a drainage mat) with a permeable drainage pipe is also an option.

Gabion baskets are made of rectangular wire meshing, spot-welded and held together with clips or spirals. Intermediate walls and spacer elements stiffen the baskets. The meshing, walls and spacers are all made of galvanized aluminum wire.

Gabions should preferably be filled by hand. Different mesh sizes and wire strengths allow mechanical filling as well as filling with different materials (for example, the extruded crushed glass product Misapor). The aesthetic of the wall will change correspondingly. Fine mesh sizes or double mesh systems emphasize the metal mesh more than larger meshes. As a basic rule, the fill material must match the mesh size!

Ready-filled gabions have recently also become available. The ready-to-go gabion baskets come straight from the quarry where they are filled right on vibrator plates. They are made using 6 to 8 millimeters wire, often combined with flat-bar steel, and can therefore be made very large, and lifted and transported once filled. This new generation of gabions makes sense for large sites with simple geometries. Adjustment on site is not possible. When there is poor access to a site or complex layout geometries need to be built, the unfilled gabions are the better option.

Peter Geitz, landscape architect and bioengineering specialist, writes: "Gabions should contain both soil and vegetation so that the empty spaces between the rocks can support growth, increasing both their aesthetic and ecological value. We plant layers of shrubs, hedges or shrubs and hedges, as was once common practice, between the layers of gabions. The gabions are thus grown through with roots and hold together better long-term, even if the wire should rust through." (Peter Geitz, Geitz & Partner GbR, 16 October 2007)

Fig. 8.28: Construction concept of a gabion retaining wall by SYTEC.

Fig. 8.29: Gabions in a garden.

Stone Block Walls

Stone block walls are walls made from big, flat-surfaced blocks. For large heights they are combined with nailing (cuts) and reinforcement (fills). Stone block walls require gravel and sand aggregate foundations.

Pre-cast Element Retaining Walls

Planted pre-cast retaining elements belong to the gravity wall group and are only suitable for heights of up to 4 meters because of their narrow width. Pre-cast retaining wall systems are found in almost every construction material catalogue. Their appearance is generally problematic.

Fig. 8.30 left: A stone block wall acts as the embankment retaining element adjacent to a garage entrance.

Fig. 8.31 right: Vegetated retention elements in a new housing development. Poor design is the price of maximum use.

Natural Stone Retaining Walls

Natural stone walls with concrete backing are most commonly found in mountain regions. The backing concrete is poured as the front stone cladding is built up. The wall should be composed of at least 30% connector stones (24 centimeters thick and interlocking at least 10 centimeters into the concrete). The reinforcement should be calculated by a structural engineer. Walls up to 1 meter high can be built as dry stone walls.

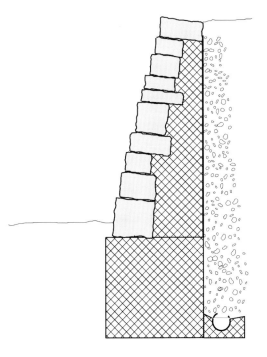

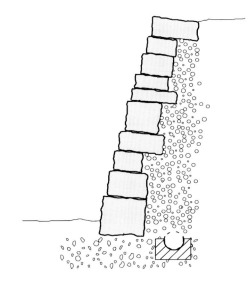

Fig. 8.32 top left: Natural stone wall with concrete backing.

Fig. 8.33 top right: Dry stone wall.

Fig.8.34 below: A natural stone wall at Frank Lloyd Wright's Fallingwater in Pennsylvania.

Grading on the Construction Site

Long before the mechanization of the construction industry, a level was an essential part of every landscaper's basic tools. In 1788, the famous landscape gardener Humphry Repton used grading and surveying as the theme for his business card. Repton had 1000 copies printed. Each showed an image of him standing behind a builder's level, giving instructions to a team of busy diggers. An exhausted employee rests behind Repton, holding a measuring rod. The engraving beautifully shows how, long before the existence of excavators and cultivators, surveying instruments were the precursors of mechanization in landscaping.

Staking Out with GPS Instruments

GPS instruments can be very useful when staking out. In 2003, landscape architecture students at the University of Applied Sciences Rapperswil demonstrated the potential of staking out using GPS. As part of the Land Art Project, which celebrated the 200th anniversary of the founding of Canton St. Gallen, the students translated 13 artists' sketches into landscape art projects in the Swiss Rhine Valley. The original sketches were digitalized and defined using regional coordinates. This new data was saved onto GPS instruments and used by the students in the field to stake out. The seeds of lupins, corn, wheat and so on were spread using agricultural sowing machinery. Whoever walked along the flanks of the Upper Rhine valley, or took the cable car up the mountain, was able to clearly see the Land Art pictures. The sketches were even clearly recognizable in satellite images taken from altitudes of 600 kilometers.

Staking Out with a Tacheometer

A tacheometer is an easy-to-use survey instrument developed especially for the construction industry. Either two coordinate points or a construction axis with one elevation must be known to set up the tacheometer correctly on site. Simple menu functions such as "stake out" enable proposed structures to be located horizontally (plan) and vertically (elevation). An additional drawing providing a reference axis, existing and proposed spot elevations is a useful orientation guide on site. Currently, only very expensive survey tacheometers provide fully automatic self-positioning.

Fig. 9.1 top left: Engraving by Thomas Medland: Humphry Repton's business card.

Fig. 9.2 top right: In Vilters, the artist Sepp Azzola's "earth person" welcomed visitors with a 350 m wide hug. In June, the earth person's laugh was green; in July, wheat-gold. For a brief period in mid-summer, the earth person even greeted the sky with blue, lupin eyes.

Fig. 9.3 bottom left: A University of Applied Sciences Rapperswil student and a farmer using GPS to stake out a Land Art picture. A collage was made to make the picture easier to visualize. Even in clear weather, the GPS satellites which transmit the positioning data are not visible to the naked eye.

Fig. 9.4 bottom right: University of Applied Sciences Rapperswil students setting out using a Leica Geosystems "Builder".

Fig.9.5: The so-called "drawing rod" with an iron tip, was used in the 19th century to help stake out (Sckell 1825, Tab i).

"When a garden is apparently or actually flat, this monotonous, lifeless form can be brought closer to the picturesque if gentle rises are formed at appropriate places, creating neither hills nor valleys, but giving the morbid flatness movement and life. Similar improvements and additions may even give the garden a pictorial value, so that it becomes an ornament. Such rises, even if they are only 1, 2 or 3 feet are often ample enough to break up a monotonous area and relay such variety as to offer much pleasure and agreeableness." (Sckell 1825, p. 88–89)

ASCII-Punktehaufen.txt – Construction Data Manager (Meter)			
Datei Bearbeiten ?			

| Sende zum Instrument | | Empfange vom Instrument | |

Punktnummer	Ost	Nord	Höhe
1	641297.270	215608.990	785.550
2	641310.000	215610.000	786.320
3	641325.000	215610.000	787.510
4	641343.260	215611.920	789.340
5	641355.000	215610.000	789.070
6	641370.000	215610.000	789.870
7	641385.000	215610.000	789.390
8	641400.000	215610.000	789.480
9	641416.530	215607.280	787.220
10	641430.000	215610.000	784.930
11	641449.980	215612.020	781.710
12	641457.830	215610.000	780.360
13	641475.000	215610.000	777.780
14	641486.640	215615.990	775.430
15	641503.620	215610.180	771.910
16	641522.810	215610.270	766.180
17	641535.000	215610.000	762.040
18	641546.890	215609.430	757.650
19	641565.000	215610.000	751.280
20	641580.000	215610.000	745.790
21	641595.000	215610.000	741.110
22	641610.000	215610.000	737.890

Wooden Stakes and Profile Aids

Staking out usually produces a chaotic array of marker stakes. What is the correct procedure for staking out? Wooden posts, referenced to a local benchmark, define a reference elevation. These wooden posts are placed somewhat outside of the actual grading area, with the reference benchmark elevation marked with a nail. To show the actual proposed grading line within the grading field, contractors flag smaller stakes with colored ribbon or paint them to make cut or fill easier to identify. Red is used to show cut, blue to show fill and red and blue at "daylight points" where there is no cut or fill. A corresponding numerical indication is typically also written directly onto the stake, for example – 0.35 meters indicates cut on a cut stake, or + 0.35 meters means fill on a fill stake. +/- 0.00 will be written on a no cut / no fill stake. Daylight points may occur at the perimeter of the grading site where the existing elevation of the surroundings is met or in areas where the proposed ground line passes through the existing ground line. There are, however, no standard guidelines for staking techniques, and the methods used differ from one contractor to another.

Wooden crossbar profiles are used to set out slopes and cut or fill embankments. These are generally a wooden crossbar nailed to two wooden posts, where the top edge of the crossbar (profile board) defines the top edge of the slope of the proposed incline. On long embankments they are placed at 2 to 5 meter intervals. The terms "embankment aid" and "profile aid" are synonyms for a crossbar profile. Modern excavators can program the angle of excavation directly into their digger's control panel, replacing the need for such stationary profile aids.

A builder's level is used to define the crossbar profile angle and check embankment angles. Here too, digital laser instruments are increasingly replacing traditional analog instruments.

Fig. 9.6 left: ASCII data of the proposed elevations, ready for transfer to a tacheometer via USB.

Fig. 9.7 right: Traditional staking out with a tape measure, measuring rod and angle prism is gradually being superseded by more modern technology in landscape construction.

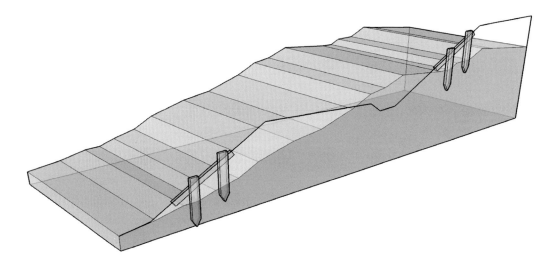

Fig. 9.8 top left: A stake with the grading elevation.

Fig. 9.9 top right: A laser instrument shows slope in percent or degrees.

Fig. 9.10 bottom: Wooden crossbar profiles indicate the proposed embankment grading line.

Fig. 9.11 top: Wooden stakes and embankment aids were used during the grading of the project "Chilenbach". First, the excavator driver dug a trench with the projected channel floor depth and width. The posts on either side of the trench were colored to provide orientation for the subsequent excavation work.

Fig. 9.12 center: The proposed angle of the embankment was repeatedly checked with a mobile level.

Fig. 9.13 bottom: The "Chilenbach" channel is integrated into the landscape and drains off surplus water.

Site Grading Construction Machinery

The first excavators where developed in the mid-19th century. These early machines ran on tracks, were powered by steam engines, and were used to excavate brown coal in open-cast mines. In about 1912, the company Caterpillar introduced continuous tracks for excavation diggers of up to 60 tons. This new mobility technology made the machines significantly quicker, and spread rapidly throughout the industry. The first walking excavators came onto the market soon after. Walking excavators still have the advantage of being able to work on soft ground and on difficult sites. However, the real revolution happened in 1970. Up to then, the digger arm had been controlled via cables, which ran to the motor on rollers; a common but tricky mechanism. In contrast, the motor of a hydraulic excavator drives a pump, which is controlled by valves, and pressurizes oil into tubes. At the end of these tubes is a cylinder with a piston rod that moves in and out. Since its introduction, hydraulic technology has firmly established itself. As in the automobile industry, electronics also play an increasingly important role in the next generation of excavation machinery.

The following pages give a designer's insight into the basic properties of the machines that excavate, load, transport and compact soil. The machine profiles are based on information provided by Marco Riva, managing director of the landscape, road and civil contracting company Toller AG in Eschenbach, Switzerland.

Fig. 9.14: Paul Albanese, golf course architect and director of golf course architecture at Edinburgh College of Art, restored the bunkers of the Christiana Creek Country Club in Elkhart, USA, using 19th-century construction machinery: two heavy Belgian workhorses, harnessed to a plow.

Fig. 9.15 top right: Hydraulics revolutionized excavation technology.

Fig. 9.16 top left: Menk steam excavator, built in 1927, 50–55 t. Three people were needed to operate the excavator (driver, stoker, and greaser). The Menk steam excavator was the first universal excavator, and could be fitted with excavation and shovel buckets, a grappler, or dozerblade. It was bolted and riveted toghether (‹monsterbagger.de›).

Fig. 9.17 bottom: The 27.5 t Menk MA (built in 1938) is Germany's oldest functioning cable excavator. It resides at the Monster Excavator Park (Monsterbagger-Park) near Bamberg.

Machinery for Soil Excavation and Loading

Type   *Capacity*
Compact excavator /
Mini-digger m^3 10
0.8–2.5 m^2 100

— Small earth moving
— Light to mid-weight soils
— Can be used in tight spaces
— Replaces manual work
— Used for backfilling (walls, structures)
— Site grading in domestic gardens

Fig. 9.18

Type   *Capacity*
Small excavator m^3 100
3.0–9.0t m^2 500

— Civil engineering works
— Medium-sized earthworks in domestic and
  housing developments
— Light to mid-weight soils
— Minimal ground pressure, good climbing
  ability, good terrain mobility
— Fine grading

Fig. 9.19

Type   *Capacity*
Hydraulic excavator m^3 200 to 30,000
10–40 t m^2 500 to 100,000

— Light to heavy soils
— Rock excavation
— Large-scale earth removal
— Excavation with direct loading
— Leveling with mechanical control system
— Efficient leveling performance with the
  level bucket

Fig. 9.20

Type	Capacity
Wheel excavator	m³ 1000
7–24 t	m² 50 to 2000

— Limited application in earthworks due to the
   soil pressure of the wheels
— Can drive on roads
— High mobility
— Light to mid-weight soils

Fig. 9.21

Type	Capacity
Walking excavator	m³ 10 to 500
5–9 t	m² 50 to 2000

— Steep and narrow sites, slope and terrace
   work
— Light to mid-weight soils
— Highly mobile, can be used on inclines up to
   45 degrees
— Some can be driven on roads
— Widely used in mountainous regions

Fig. 9.22

Type	Capacity
Track loader / Crawler-mounted loader	m³ 1000 to 20,000
	m² 0
5–30 t	

— Light to heavy soils
— Gravel quarrying, soil excavation
— Moving and loading
— Suitable only for short distances
— Optional: ripper bucket
— Optional: swamp excavator (wider tracks)

Fig. 9.23

Type
Bulldozer
5–50 t

Capacity
m³ 1000 to 100,000
m² 1000 to >100,000

— Light to heavy soils
— Moving soils, dam construction, grading
— Ski slope construction, fine grading with GPS remote control
— Rock excavation with ripper bucket
— Optional: swamp excavator (wider tracks)
— Optional: GPS/GLONASS remote control
— Optional: laser level verification

Fig. 9.24

Type
Scrapedozer

Capacity
m³ 5000 to 1,000,000
m² 0

— All-round machinery for digging, loading, and transporting
— Exerts little pressure on soil, good weight distribution
— Very economic when transportation distance lies between 50 and 500 m
— Self-loading

Fig. 9.25

Type
Scraper

Capacity
m³ 5000 to >100,000
m² 0

— Unsuitable for grading
— Needs stable soils to support wheel base
— Self-loading is an advantage
— High transportation capacity over large distances

Fig. 9.26

Type	Capacity
Grader	m³ 0
7–28 t	m² 500 to >10,000

Fig. 9.27

— Pure grading machine
— Suitable only for gravel or load stable soils
— Limited use in earthworks
— Used in construction of roads and sport surfaces (paved surfaces)
— Optional: laser control sensors for a profile accuracy of +/- 1 cm
— Optional: GPS/GLONASS machine remote control based on digital site model
— Optional: elevation measuring with ultra-sound for level verification
— Optional: cross-level sensor to verify the cross fall of roads

Machinery for Soil Transportation

Type

Wheel loader

Compact loader

3–15 t

Capacity

m³ 5 to 1000

— Loading and moving of excavation and
  loose material
— Light to mid-weight soils
— Requires high loadbearing substrate to work
  on
— Fast and highly mobile for small quantities
— Additional tools: concrete mixing bucket

Fig. 9.28

Type

Track dumper

0.3–22 t

Capacity

m³ 1 to 10,000

— Suitable for moving soil materials on low
  loadbearing soils
— Transportation distances of 5 to 500 m
— Single load 0.3–12 m³
— Good slope performance (up to 25% incline)

Fig. 9.29

Type

Small dumper

Wheel dumper

1.2–3.6 t

Capacity

m³ 1 to 100

— Application on loadbearing soil bases
— Can drive on roads
— High speed and great mobility
— Single load 1 to 2.5 m³
— Loading bay can be hydraulically turned and
  emptied

Fig. 9.30

Type	*Capacity*
Articulated dump truck	m³ 200 to 100,000

— Moving of soil, excavation and gravel materials
— Needs loadbearing soil base
— Transportation distances 100 to over 3000 m
— High speed 10–30 km/h
— High center of gravity and dumping height
— Single load 9–18 m³
— Not permitted on public roads

Fig. 9.31

Machines for Soil Compaction

Type
Trench compactor
1.5–2.5 t

Capacity
m³ 5 to 300
m² 10 to 300

— Backfilling structures and trenches
— Slim design
— High compaction coefficient
— Good slope performance characteristics
— Compaction depth max. 50–70 cm

Fig. 9.32

Type
Tandem-vibration
plate compactor
2.5–15 t

Capacity
m³ 10 to >1000
m² 10 to >1000

— Suitable for gravel subbases
— Compaction depth 20–60 cm
— Limited application in earthworks (only on level surfaces)
— Poor slope performance characteristics

Fig. 9.33

Type
Roller compactor
7–15 t

Capacity
m³ 100 to >10,000
m² 100 to >1000

— Suitable for dam and landfill works
— High compaction rate
— Good slope performance characteristics, and site mobility
— Compaction depth from 40 to 80 cm
— Optional: installed compaction measurement instruments
— Optional: pad foot drums for deep compaction

Fig. 9.34

Fig. 9.35: A GPS-controlled dozer in action.

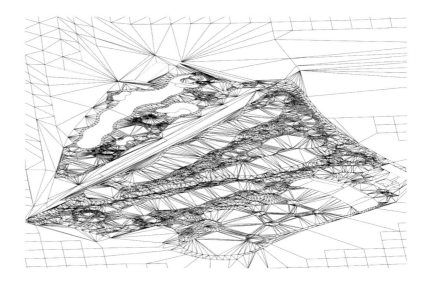

Fig. 9.35 top left: Grading a golf course in Bad Ragaz using a GPS dozer.

Fig. 9.36 top center: Bulldozer drivers prefer manual control when grading golf courses. However, using GPS they can see the exact position of their bulldozer in relation to the proposed contour lines.

Fig. 9.37 top right: The display in the dozer cabin.

Fig. 9.38 bottom: An accurate triangulation of the proposed design is needed for fully automatic grading.

GPS Remote Control in Site Grading

On large construction projects, specialized landscape and civil contractors use 3D GPS dozer technology. In addition to electronic control equipment mounted in the bulldozer, this requires a reference station (the base station) and a mobile receiver (the rover) mounted on the blade. As with a normal GPS receiver, real-time calculation of both data sets are used to establish an exact location. Even free, natural-style site grading, common in landscape and garden construction, can be carried out with accuracy to within centimeters using GPS remote control and without the demanding task of staking out the site. The grading can be either fully automatic or manual. One basic requirement, however, is that the designer provides the

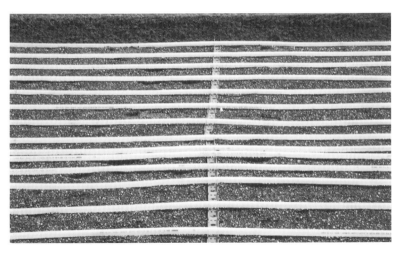

Fig. 9.40 top: The Letzigrund construction site in Zurich (spring 2007). This is one of the stadiums where UEFA EURO 2008 games will take place.

Fig. 9.41 center: The rolled sod is laid on a 12 cm soil bed and a leveling course of sand (0-4 mm, 12 cm deep). Below this is a heating system (water pipes at 12 cm intervals) and a sprinkler irrigation system.

Fig. 9.42 bottom: A GPS-controlled bulldozer was used to install the sand and soil bed, a new experience for the contractor. Even the experienced supervising foreman was astounded at the speed with which the grading works were carried out.

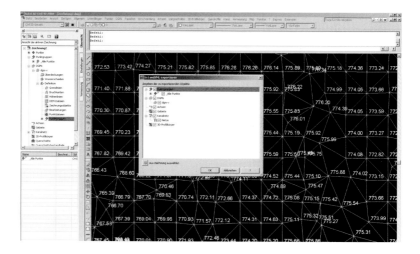

Fig. 9.43: Export of LandXML data from Autodesk Civil 3D to be used for GPS machinery remote control on a construction site.

contractor with a triangulation plan of the design, based on a digital site model of the existing site collated by a surveyor. The non-propriety software LandXML (‹landxml.org›) is the chief exchange format between CAD systems and grading machinery, and is supported by most software. The contractor's survey technician copies the data onto a flash drive, which he or she then uses to "feed" the dozer control panel on site, making staking out work redundant. The survey technician needs half an hour for work that previously required three people for half a day. Nevertheless, the accuracy of the input data is crucial. The bulldozer will get the grading right first time if the existing site data are correct. Any calculation errors in the data set will simply be carried out, thus shifting responsibility from the contractor to the designer. As a consequence, extreme care must be taken with the plan data, and in particular the initial digital site model.

GLONASS stands for global navigation satellite system. It is the Russian global satellite navigation system (GNSS) and counterpart to GPS. Systems able to receive both GPS and GLONASS are available to professionals. The better the coverage, the more reliable the data reception, and downtime on site can be avoided. Good reception is especially important when working in road ravines, the mountains, deep trenches and excavations. Galileo is the equivalent European satellite navigation system, which will come on the market within the next few years.

However, the dozer can still work in areas with no satellite reception. The embankment angles and all necessary data (which otherwise would have been defined with staking out aids and markers) are saved in the control panel. In addition, the dozer is equipped with ultrasound, which

Fig. 9.44 top: The company Westrag, based in Wollerau/ Neuhaus in Switzerland, has a Caterpillar track bulldozer, equipped with Topcon laser, ultrasound, and GPS remote control.

Fig. 9.45 center: GPS simplifies grading, in particular on open sites with few reference points.

Fig. 9.46 bottom: Westrag use their dozer to construct roads in housing developments. In such instances, the laser and ultrasound remote control systems are used.

allows manholes and curb edges to be measured without actually coming into contact with them, thus establishing a reference datum. Furthermore, laser grading of, for example, sport grounds and parking lots is another automatic positioning method where a rotational laser pilots the dozer. Elevation and cross fall corrections are sent via the hydraulics directly to the grading machinery. The driver steers by the control panel display, which shows the exact position, slope, and contour line. This system is easy to handle and can be learnt quickly – the value of which should not be underestimated on a construction site.

Typically, such highly advanced construction machinery tends to be used on bigger projects. Access roads, parking lots and lawn areas are already the conventional domain of the dozer. Earthworks without surveying, or the direct implementation of 3D plans, are common practice – the interaction of surveying and grading is not always problem-free. Typically, once the manual setting out has been completed, marking stakes then get driven over. The surveyor has to come again and may not immediately be available, which causes delay and downtime when grading machinery just sits around on site. These are important arguments why automatic intelligent positioning systems are currently also being used on excavators. Construction professionals who have already worked with GPS remote control swear by it. They are convinced that the combination of construction machinery remote control with digital site models generated by the designer will play an increasingly important role in civil engineering in the near future.

Fig. 9.47: It can be anticipated that in near future the use of GPS remote control systems with excavators will become more commonplace.

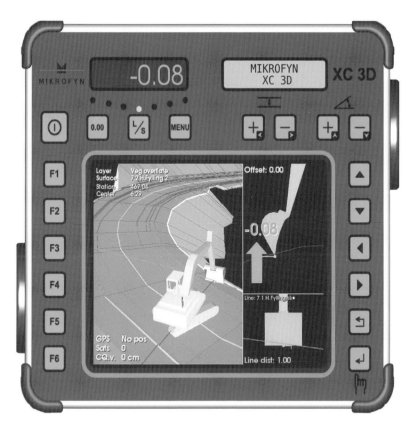

Fig. 9.48: View of the Visual-DiggerTM control panel in the driver's cabin.

Practical Examples

A landscape architect's work combines ecological, technical and design knowledge with the ability to think laterally and perform planning tasks. Landscape architects work on various scale levels. While landscape planning entails the analysis, evaluation and formulation of recommendations for entire regions, landscape architecture encompasses the design and construction documentation of public and private open space, parks and gardens. For this chapter "Practical Examples", a selection of projects from two offices was chosen from both ends of the scale, with an emphasis on site grading.

Harradine Golf / Orient Irrigation Services

Site grading is a major component of every golf course design project. Golf course architects design with contours and build with soil. For this reason, the chosen protagonist for this chapter is a company that for many years has specialized in golf courses and gardens. In 1929, Don Harradine founded the company Harradine Golf in Switzerland, and designed numerous projects. In 1976 his son Peter opened a branch office in Dubai and now runs the company from there. Peter Harradine subsequently founded a partner company called Orient Irrigation Services in 1977, likewise with its main headquarters in Dubai. Orient Irrigation Services performs the technical design and drawing of irrigation and pump systems, coordinates plant deliveries from several nurseries, and carries out contracting services. Three projects by these two firms ideally illustrate practical site grading under unusual circumstances.

A Golf Course

The Al Hamra Golf Course is in Ras al-Khaimah, one of the seven states of the United Arab Emirates. Its proximity to the ocean and desert location provided Peter Harradine with the design concept for the "Seaside Desert Golf Course". Salty soils proved a particular challenge during the construction of the 18-hole course. To improve growing conditions for the plants, large machinery was used to move enormous quantities of sand so that the actual design grading could take place on a base of sweet sand, on average of 3 meters thick. The term "sweet sand" refers to sand imported from the country's interior, which has a lower salt content. It is only thanks to this improved soil medium and large quantities of freshwater that the planted palms and lawns are able to survive in the extreme climate conditions.

Fig. 10.1: Detail excerpt from the Al Harm Golf Course Grading Plan.

The top 20 to 30 centimeters of sand were mixed with a soil activator (soil organisms in a compost extract) and clay granules to improve water retention. The holes dug for the date and coconut palms were 2 x 2 meters, and the soil was improved with added fertilizer.

Imagine you want to build a sandcastle with dry sand – you won't have much fun because sand can only be shaped when it is damp. The sweet sand was therefore sprayed with water before it was graded. Trucks with large water tanks are part of every grading contractor's basic machinery in this region. Once the sand had been wet, bulldozers were able to grade the complex shapes called for by the design.

The salt-tolerant grass Sea Isle 2000 Paspalum is able to form a closed sod suitable for golf greens. Nevertheless, the grass and palms need constant irrigation, or they will simply dry out. Salt extraction plants provide this irrigation water. Drip irrigation pipes deliver water to the palms, and sprinklers are used for the fairways and greens.

Computers are naturally amongst the staff's basic tools. Site data collection and modeling are increasingly done using GPS. Cut and fill volumes and profiles were calculated using a digital site model. Peter Harradine still places great value on his staff being able to master certain analog skills, such as hand sketching designs with contour lines.

Fig. 10.2: Sweet sand needs to be watered before it is graded.

Fig. 10.3 top: Peter Harradine on site. Despite detailed construction documents, active construction supervision is vital to ensure a successfully executed project.

Fig. 10.4 bottom: Hole 7 at the Al Hamra Golf Course shortly after completion.

A Private Garden

A private garden designed by Heiko Heinig, landscape architect and director of the design department of Orient Irrigation Services, is located on
the outskirts of Dubai. The architect and landscape architect developed the
house and garden concept together. Rather than one big central building,
as would be typical for the region, several pavilion style buildings fulfill
living, dining, and sleeping room functions.

The client wanted to keep the existing sloped topography and have
water as the main design element. Wooden decks, lightly layered over
one another, bridge the changes of level and connect the pavilions that
lie staggered through the steep site. Through clever site grading, a small
stream flows harmoniously between water feature elements scattered
around the pavilions to a lake at the lowest point of the garden. Costs
played a secondary role.

Fig. 10.5: A grading plan was
a key requirement for the
successful implementation of
the project.

The lake is not just a special eye-catcher. Should the public water supply be cut off, it functions as an emergency water reserve. Tanks are normally used for this purpose; they should be able to store one day's worth of water. This security is needed as plants in this climate simply die if they are not irrigated. The plants have a high water demand. A palm tree needs about 180 liters of water per day, deciduous trees about 90 liters. Shrubs and lawns are watered with 12 l/m^2 per day in high summer.

For many reasons, this was a complex project. The designer mastered the challenge only thanks to a detailed grading concept with contour lines and spot elevations.

Fig. 10.6 top: Using the simplest tools, workers compact the water feature surfaces. The sand was wet before being worked.

Fig. 10.7 bottom: Wooden decks bridge the water features and connect the various pavilion levels.

Fig. 10.8 right: The palm avenue on the lightly sloped lawn at the entrance is a calming contrast to the playful water landscapes of the eastern part of the garden.

Fig. 10.9 and 10.10: The waterfall and lake are a real eye-catcher. The lake is also an emergency reservoir for irrigation water.

An Island

This private island near Dubai is one of the world's most well-known artificial islands. It has received huge publicity in the media and can easily be found on Internet map services. The island's name and client shall remain anonymous. The landscape architect in charge of the project at Orient Irrigation Services, Heiko Heinig, describes the design task as: "Creating space on the island for both private use and prestigious events". The island lies 3 meters above sea level. A water axis cuts through the free landform and emphasizes the change in level through water steps. The total construction costs shall likewise not be mentioned. They were very high, even by Dubai standards.

How does one build a dream island? A brief introduction:
- Dredgers deliver sand and rock and dump it into a marked water area until a stable underwater subbase is established.
- Special ships blow material, sucked up from the ocean floor several kilometers away, out of their holds. This is called "rainbowing". A sand hill is gradually created above sea level.
- Machinery grades sweet sand to create the surface landforms, following the landscape architects' design plans. The improved sand is laid to an average depth of 1.5 meters.
- Metal elements protect shore sections open to the ocean from wave action and erosion.

Fig. 10.12: Aerial photograph of Dubai from the Image Science and Analysis Laboratory, NASA-Johnson Space Center. "The Gateway to Astronaut Photography of Earth."

Fig. 10.13 and 10.14 right: "Rainbowing" an island on the coast of Dubai.

The high costs were generated by material transportation and complex logistics. Each tree and shrub had to be delivered by ship. A journey by speedboat took at least 40 minutes, heavy ships took much longer. A

desalination plant was installed on the island to provide freshwater for irrigation; a water treatment plant cleansed grey water for reuse. The selection of plants, already quite reduced in Dubai because of the climate, is even further limited by the close proximity of the ocean. The key salt-tolerant vegetation planted included the grass Paspalum ssp. and date and coconut palms.

Despite the fact that economics and sustainability played no active role in the project, it remains impressive in design and technical terms. The assessment criteria of site grading (ecology, economy, technology and design) should be evaluated according to the region and culture. Keeping track of this and other similar projects therefore remains interesting. The cost of energy will eventually rise in the Arab world too, and climate protection will become an important subject. Solar chimney power plants or high-tech solar panels will power the irrigation of modern, artificial oases. Financing will probably not be a problem.

Fig. 10.15: The difference in elevation between the highest land point and sea level is 3 m.

Fig. 10.16 top: The long-distance transportation of materials made construction expensive.

Fig. 10.15 center: Date palms planted in "sweet sand".

Fig. 10.16 bottom: Foundation works being carried out on the island.

ilu AG Ingenieure, Landschaftsarchitekten, Umweltfachleute

Iilu AG Ingenieure, Landschaftsarchitekten, Umweltfachleute (Engineers, Landscape Architects and Environmental Specialists) was founded in 1973 in Uster near Zurich. Experts in landscape planning, landscape management, resource management and environmental protection, the office strives to provide innovative and sustainable solutions that are both environmentally and economically sound.

ilu currently employs a staff of 12 in their two offices in Uster and Horw, including specialists in landscape architecture, landscape management, cultural and environmental engineering, geography, GIS and administration. Depending on the project, they also collaborate with various external specialists (for example, geologists, biologists, limnologists, civil and forestry engineers, geotechnicians etc., as well as with universities of applied sciences). The team offers professional services in consultancy, concept development, project proposals, planning permission and construction supervision, with particular emphasis on:

- Project coordination
- Waste management: landfill design and proposals, toxic waste reclamation
- Resource supply: excavation projections, resource management
- Hydraulic engineering, water management, water conservation, road runoff treatment
- Environmental impact studies
- Landscape conservation planning
- Open space planning
- Geoinformatics (GIS), application development

Fig. 10.19 left: ilu staff.

Fig. 10.20 right: An ilu workstation.

The office has used the latest information technology in GIS and CAD since the end of the 1980s, and as such has pioneered the use of IT in landscape architecture in Switzerland. Logically, considering the main focus of their work, digital terrain models are at the heart of the GIS and CAD work being carried out in the office. The fields at application for digital site models at ilu include:

- Modeling resource excavation and landfill proposals
- Volume calculations
- Generating profiles
- Modeling proposed project area grading
- 3D visualization
- Photo-realistic visualizations

The broad range of possible applications for digital terrain modeling is illustrated below in the Reuss delta project and two quarry extension visualization projects.

Fig. 10.21: Study of a landfill as an acoustic barrier. The digital model served as the basis for the noise distribution calculations.

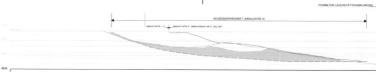

Reuss Delta

The termination of the Reuss delta gravel and sand excavation concession in 1983 opened up the opportunity to redevelop the landscape development plan for the area. Gravel excavation had been carried out close to the shore, causing large-scale shore erosion and loss of land. In addition, the original shallow water zone had been partly destroyed. The correction of the river Reuss in the mid-19th century had in fact only increased local erosion problems.

Restoration measures undertaken 20 years ago were a good start and have helped reintroduce hydrodynamic delta accumulation processes. In parallel, ilu carried out a sensitive concept study, exploring the potential for further resource extraction while improving the delta habitat. Extensive dropping of tunnel excavation material has allowed the creation of large, flat water zones and islands.

Terrain modeling, based on a lake bottom survey, was used in a variety of ways in this project.

Fig. 10.22 top: Aerial photograph of the Reuss Delta, 2006.

Fig. 10.23 bottom: A profile created automatically from the digital site model.

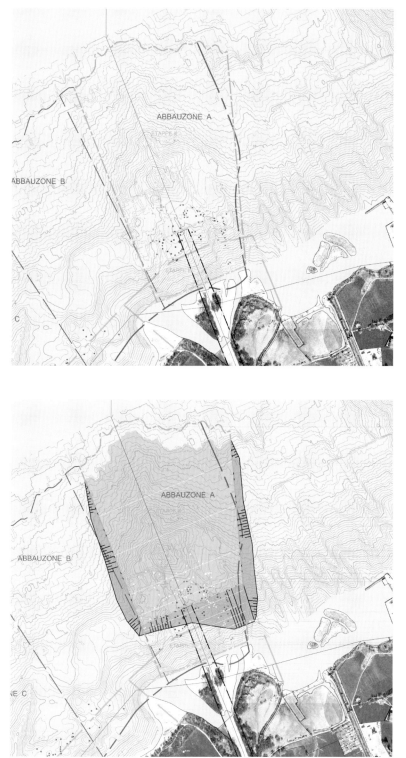

Fig. 10.22 top: Lake bottom survey with contour lines.

Fig. 10.23 bottom: Contour lines with integrated excavation floor.

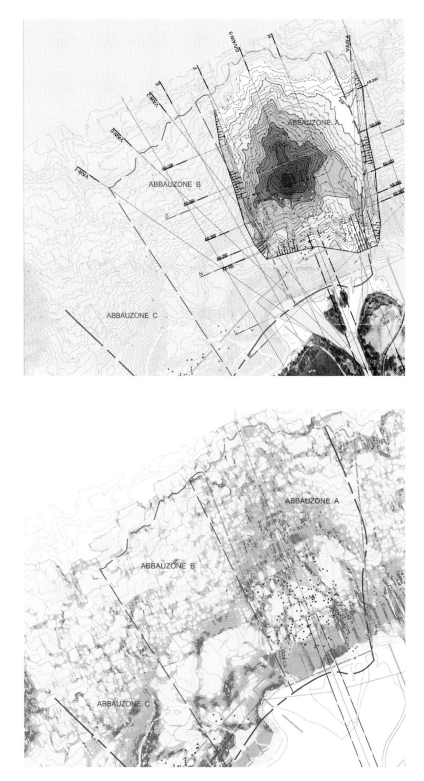

Fig. 10.26 top: Difference model with the degree of excavation.

Fig. 10.27 bottom: A map with slope classification based on the digital terrain model.

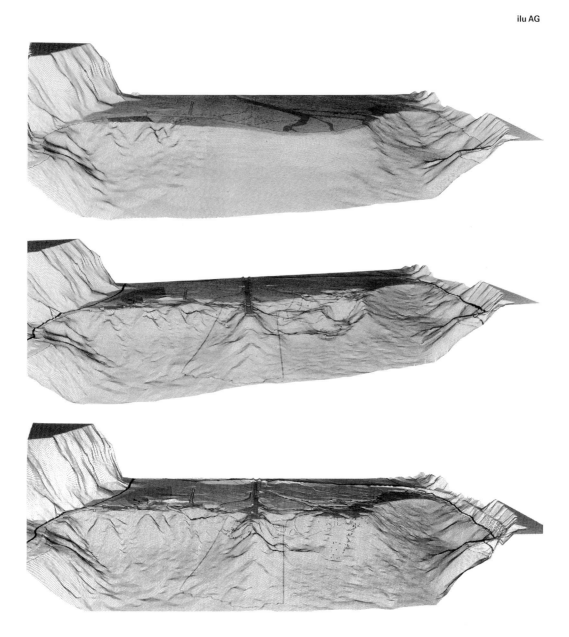

Fig. 10.28 top: 3D lake bottom representation of the Reuss Delta, 1843.

Fig. 10.29 center: 3D lake bottom representation of the Reuss Delta, 1987.

Fig. 10.30 bottom: 3D lake bottom representation of the Reuss Delta with the "Lake Fill" project, 1993.

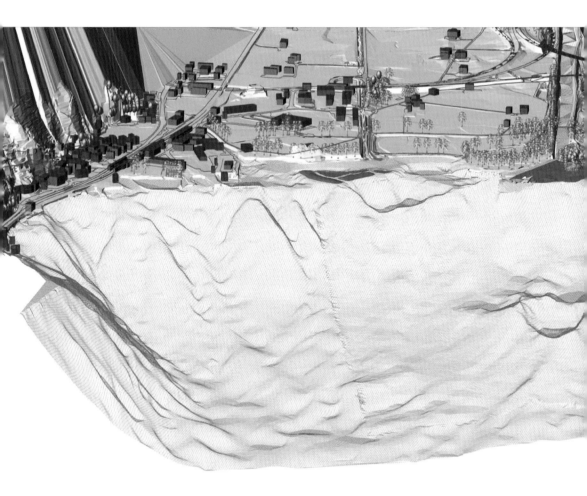

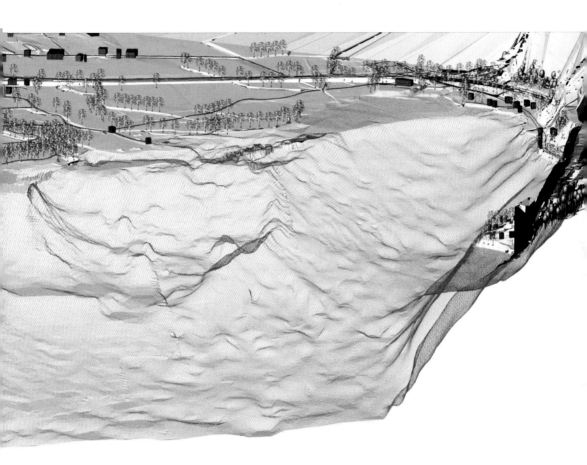

Fig. 10.31: Visualization of
the Reuss Delta, 2005.

3D Visualizations of the Netstal Quarry

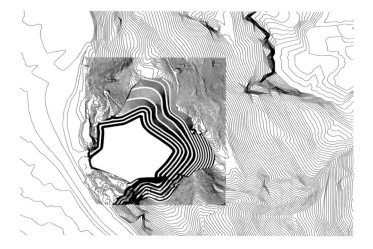

Fig. 10.32 top: 3D visualization of the Netstal quarry (Kalkfabrik Netstal AG) viewed from a prescribed perspective, "before" photograph.

Fig. 10.33 center: The proposed excavation (square with darker contour lines) integrated into the Swiss digital terrain model 1:25,000 (DHM25).

Fig. 10.34 bottom: Visualization of a possible final "after" situation based on the DTM.

Photomontage of the Zingel Quarry

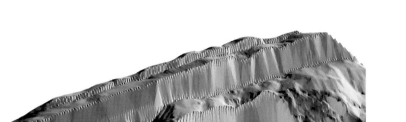

Fig. 10.35 top: Visualization study for the extension of the Zingel quarry, KIBAG Kies Seewen. The photo shows the "before" state.

Fig. 10.36 center: A digital model from the same perspective is the basis for photo-realistic retouching of the possible finished state.

Fig. 10.37 bottom: Visualization of the possible "after" situation, based on the DTM.

Appendix

Site Grading Exercises

These site grading exercises were developed by Professor Sadik C. Artunc, FASLA. As of January 2007, he is Department Head of the department of Landscape Architecture at Mississippi State University (MSU). He has previously taught landscape architecture at Louisiana State University. Professor Artunc is a registered landscape architect in the USA, a qualified forestry engineer (Istanbul University), and holds a Master of Landscape Architecture from the University of Michigan.

In the USA, a landscape architecture state license can be obtained by passing an exam composed of several parts. Site grading skills are tested in a designated section of their own. From 1984 to 1997 Professor Artunc was a member of the Landscape Architecture Registration Examination (LARE) examination committee of the Council of Landscape Architectural Registration Boards (CLARB). He developed over 1,500 exam questions for written and drawn parts of the exam during this time. As chair of the LARE committee of the American Society of Landscape Architects, he currently conducts exam preparation workshops throughout the USA.

Building with Entrance Drive
The brief:
Complete the site grading for a building and entrance drive.

Requirements:
— Rainwater from the roof and paved surfaces must be infiltrated on site, or may be conveyed to a swale, which may then run along the road. A concrete culvert pipe, with minimum top cover of 50 cm, may conduct water under the entrance drive.
— Grated U-drains collect water from the drive and disperse it directly into the surrounding site.
— Access to the building is without steps.
— Maximum embankment slope is 2:3.

- Swales must have a floor width of 1.5 m and a minimum longitudinal slope of 1%.
- Existing trees must be retained and protected. A protection zone of the crown extent + 1.50 m must be provided for.
- Contour lines should be shown with 1 m intervals.
- Important spot elevations and gradients should be indicated.

Note: Because of the small scale, this should be treated as a conceptual exercise. Indications for swale parting peaks should be given.

A Ramp

The brief:

A new set of steps and accessibility ramp are to be built at a retirement home.

Requirements:

- Rainwater runoff from the roof and paved surfaces should flow to the pond to the south.
- Grated U-drains collect water from the paving and convey it laterally onto the site.
- Maximum grade for the ramps is 6%.
- Swale floors should be represented with a dashed line.
- Maximum embankment slope 1:3.
- The contour line interval should be 0.5 m. Spot levels should be provided at important points.
- The manhole in the middle of the ramp collects water, and conveys it to the pond via an underground pipe.

Fig. 11.1 left: A pocket calculator, straight edge or even better a triangle, pencil and eraser – the tools of analog site grading design.

Fig. 11.2 right: University of Applied Sciences Rapperswil students busy with a site grading exercise.

An Acoustic Earth Wall Barrier

The brief:

A new path is to be built to a lookout platform (shown by hatching). An earth wall should offer acoustic remediation for a busy road to the west (not shown on the plan) and visually separate the lookout from the parking lot.

Requirements:
— The earth wall may be a maximum of 4 m high.
— Path rainwater should be infiltrated to the side.
— Maximum embankment slope 1:3.
— Contour lines should be shown at 1 m intervals.

Tennis Courts

The brief:

New tennis courts with a club building and terraces should be integrated into the landscape.

Requirements:
— The surface runoff should be conveyed into two swales.
— Grated U-drains collect water from the paved surfaces.
— The indicated grade on the paved surfaces must be adhered to.
— Maximum embankment slope 1:3.
— Contour lines should be shown at 1 m intervals.

Parking Lot

The brief:

A parking lot by the side of a road is to be graded.

Requirements:
— The parking lot is edged with a 10 cm wide curb.
— A debris trap collects the parking lot runoff before it is conveyed into the nearby swale.
— Indicated grades must be observed.
— Contour lines should be shown at 0.5 m intervals.

A Terraced House

The brief:

Runoff rainwater from the roof and paved surfaces should be infiltrated on site or may run into the water feature to the south.

Requirements:

— The following minimum and maximum grades must be observed:
  - entrance drive 1–5%
  - swale longitudinal axis 2–10%
  - embankments 2–33%
— Rainwater runoff from the paved surfaces may not run onto the public road.
— Contour lines should be shown at 1 m intervals.

Fig. 11.3 left: The civil engineering program Civil 3D is suitable for professional digital site modeling. Student licenses are available from students.autodesk.com.

Fig. 11.4 right: Having completed many analog site modeling exercises in the first semester, University of Applied Sciences Rapperswil students use their laptops and the CAD civil engineering program Civil 3D to create level, setting out and drainage plans in their second semester project work.

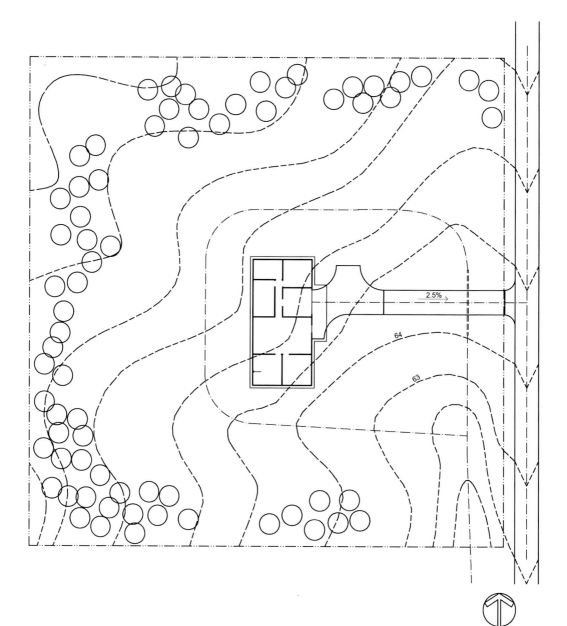

1 : 1000

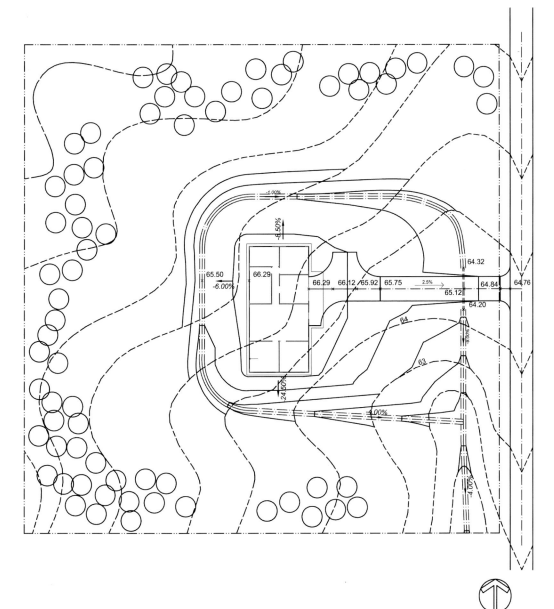

1 : 1000

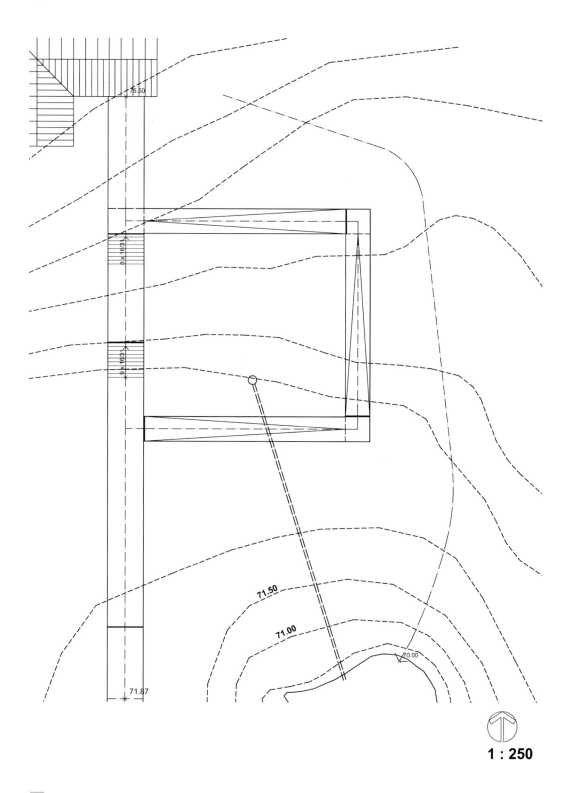

75.50

8 × 16/3

9 × 16/3

71.50

71.00

70.00

71.87

1 : 250

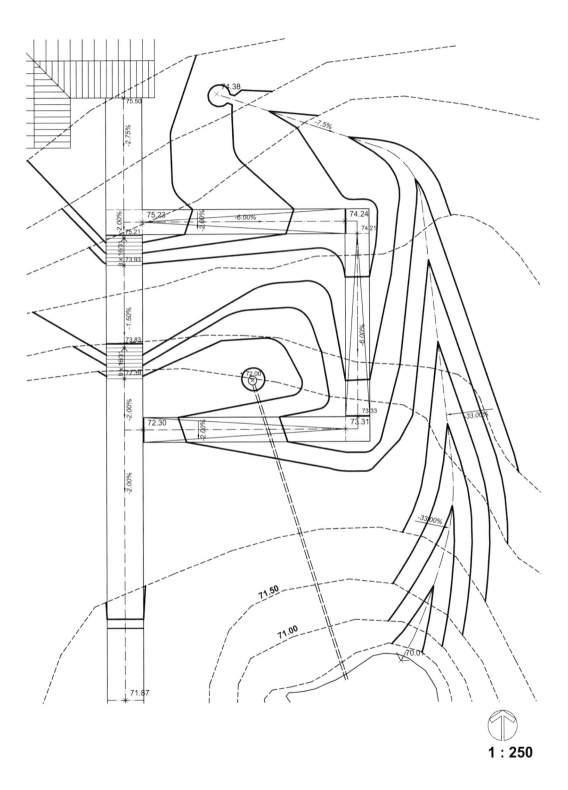

1 : 250

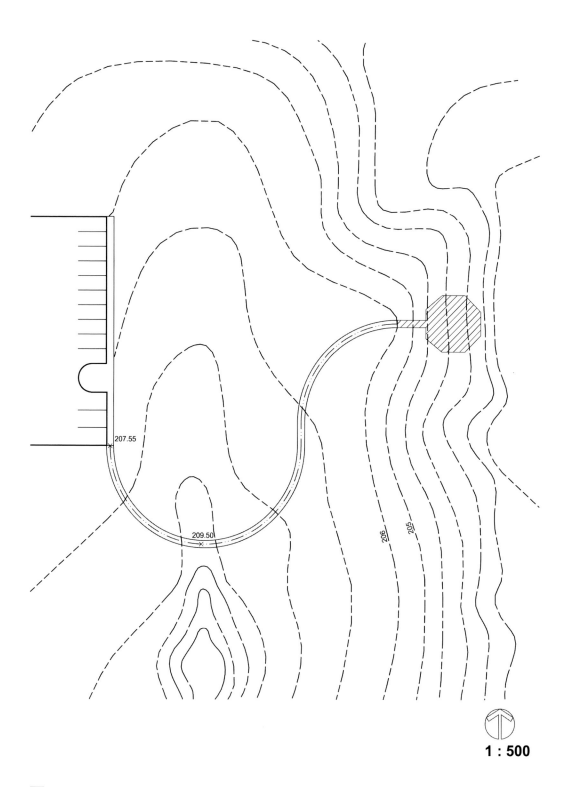

207.55

209.50

206

205

1 : 500

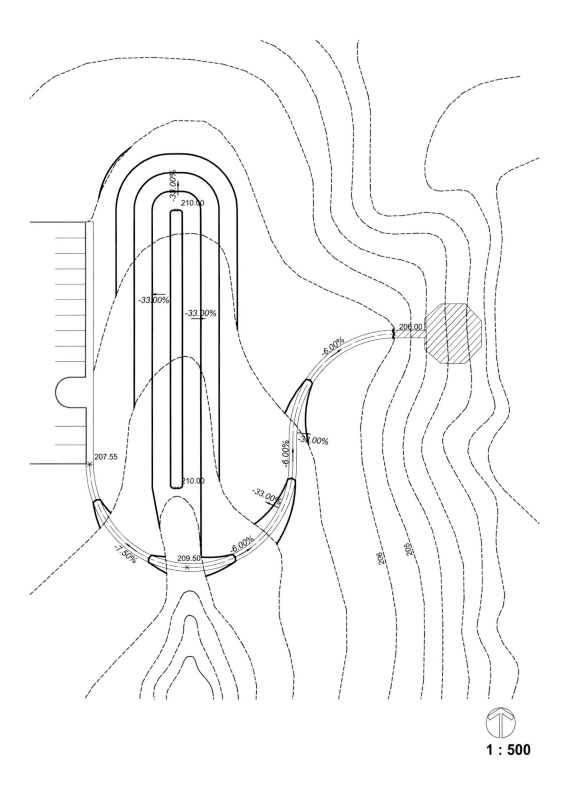

1 : 500

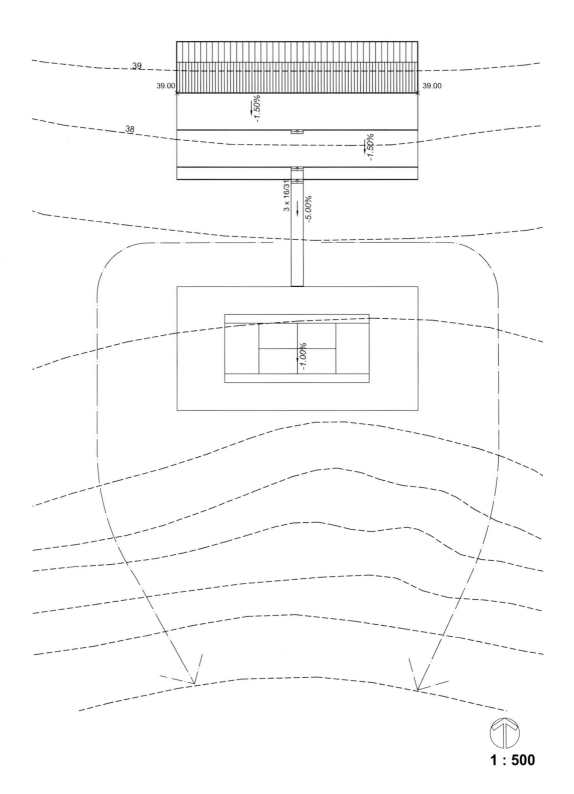

1 : 500

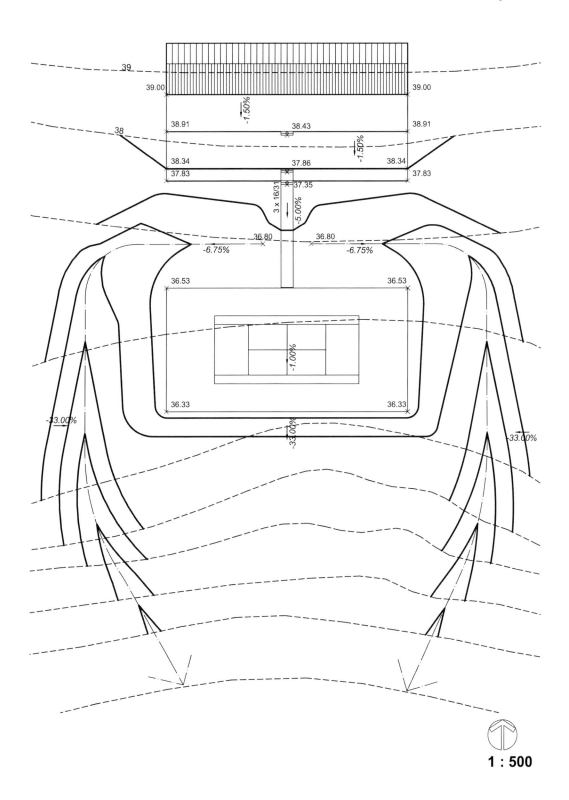

1 : 500

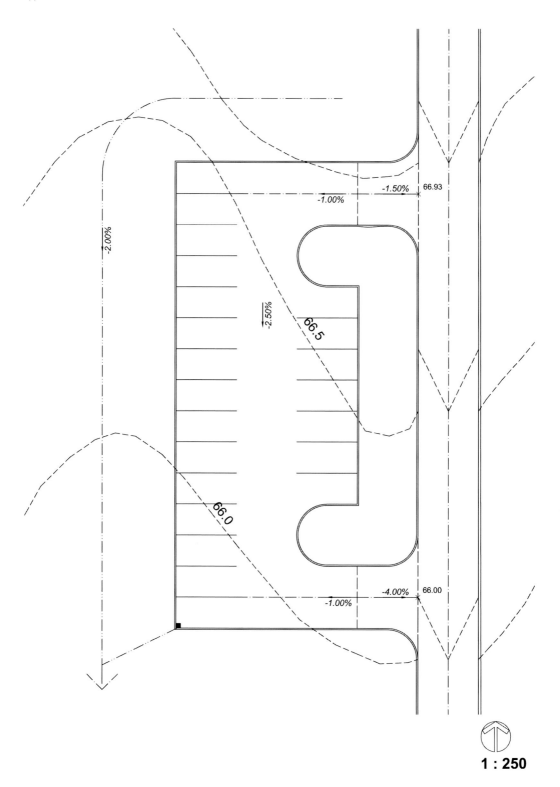

1 : 250

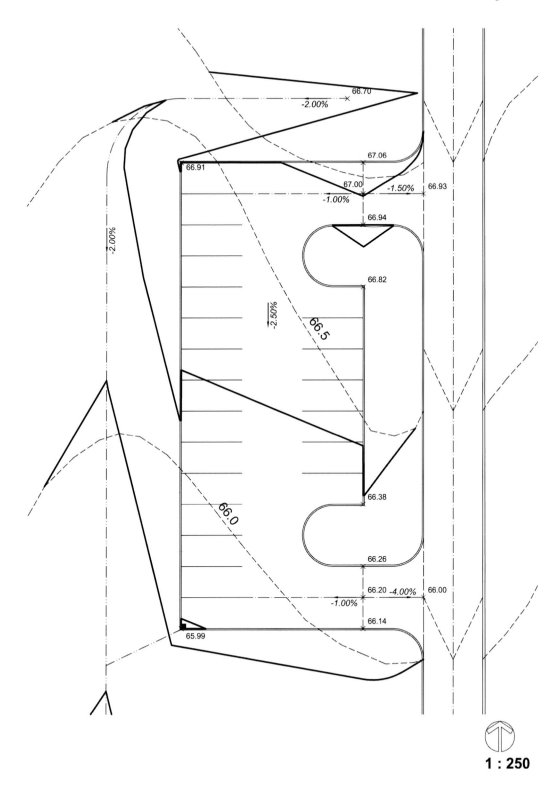

1 : 250

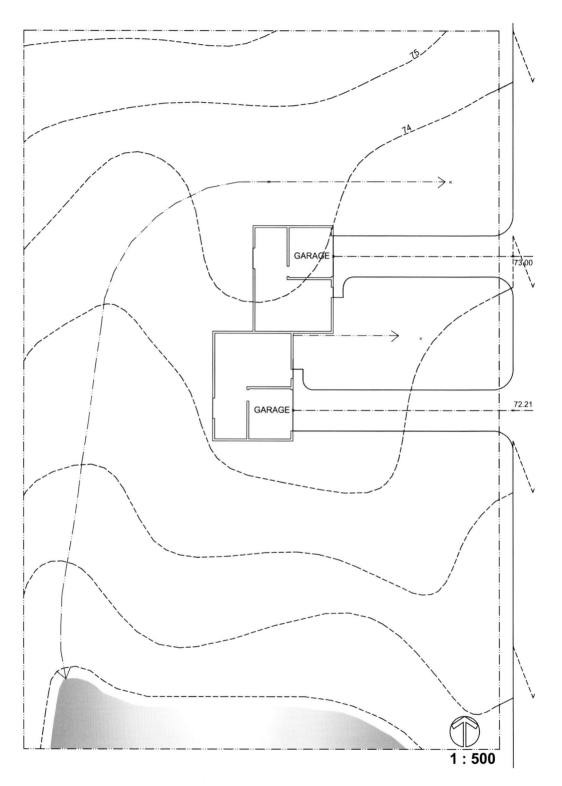

1 : 500

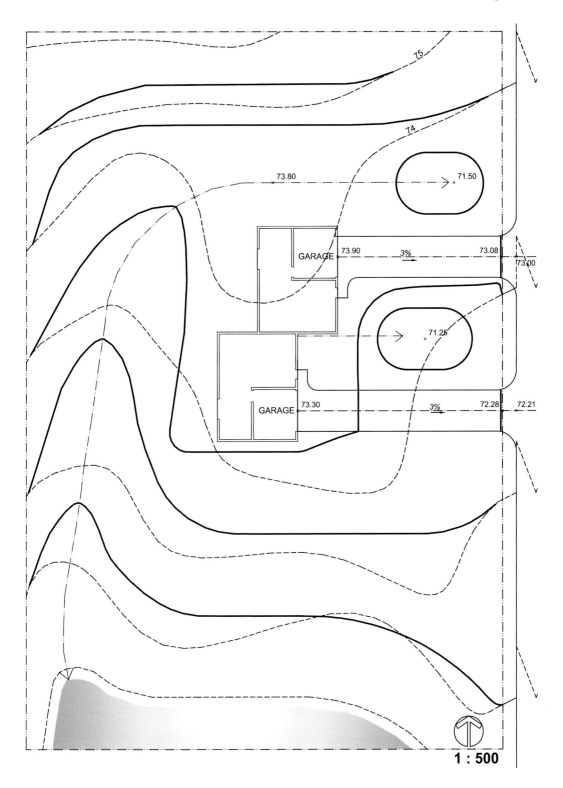

1 : 500

aggregate base

A layer of graded particulate material typically including sand and gravel, 0–32 mm diameters, laid below a finished paving surface.

aggregate subbase

A layer of graded particulate material typically including sand and gravel, 0–63 mm diameters and serving as a loadbearing layer.

alignment

The course along which the centerline of a roadway or channel is located.

angle of repose

The angle that the sloping face of a mound of loose earth, gravel or other material makes with the level horizon.

area drain

A structure for collecting runoff from relatively small, paved areas.

ASCII

American Standard Code for Information Interchange.

ASCII ArcInfo grid format

A raster of pixels, in which every pixel contains an attribute with terrain elevation data.

---

backfill

Earth or other fill material used to replace material removed during construction, such as in pipeline and culvert trenches and behind retaining walls.

base layer

A layer of specified or selected material of designed thickness, installed on the subbase or on the natural subgrade, to distribute the load and provide drainage, or on which a wearing surface or a drainage structure is planned.

base surface

Existing ground or undeveloped terrain.

bearing capacity

The load supporting capacity of a soil.

bedrock

Consolidated rock.

bench

A horizontal or sloping step in a slope.

berm

A mound of earth, often linear.

bioengineering

The discipline of pursuing technological, ecological, economic and design goals, primarily by making use of living materials, i.e. seeds, plants, parts of plants and plant communities.

breakline

In digital 3D site modeling, a line used to connect the data representing a distinct surface feature, such as a ridge line, the edge of a road, the toe of a slope, the centerline of a road, or the flowline of a ditch or stream. When a breakline is defined, the surface triangulation must first follow the breaklines, by placing triangle edges coincident with the breakline segments. This ensures that the feature is depicted accurately in the model.

borrow material

Fill material imported to a site.

borrow area

A source of earth fill material used in the construction of embankments or other earth structures.

brushlayering

Laying live branch cuttings in crisscross fashion on the benches between successive terraces of soil in embankment stabilization.

CAD

Computer Aided Design

CAM

Computer Aided Manufacturing

centerline

The survey line in the center of a road, ditch, or similar project.

compaction

The densification of a soil by a mechanical process.

contour line

An imaginary line, or its representation on a map, connecting points of the same elevation above or below a given datum.

contour interval

In a contour plan, the typical vertical distance between contour lines.

crown

The rise or difference in elevation between the edge and the centerline of a roadway.

culvert

Any structure not classified as a bridge that conveys water under a road.

cut

Soil, or other excavation material, removed in a grading operation.

cut and fill

The process of removing earth material from some locations and adding it to others by grading. The process of computing the total volume of material moved.

---

data band

A graphic frame that is associated with a profile view object or section view object. The data band contains annotations for the profile or section view, as well as for the parent horizontal alignment. Some common annotations include elevation data, stations and cut/fill depths.

datum

A reference value. All elevations or coordinates are set relative to this value. In surveying, two data (horizontal and vertical) are generally used.

debris trap

A receptacle with a sediment bowl or sump for retaining debris and fine particles before conducting surface water to a subsurface pipe.

detention basin

A structure that is normally dry and used for temporarily storing storm runoff from a drainage area to reduce the peak rate of flow.

Delaunay triangulation

A method of connecting an arbitrary set of points together in a network of triangles that meet certain mathematical criteria (specifically, the circle described by the three points in any triangle contains no other point in the set). It is used for creating a TIN.

discharge (Q)

The outflow rate through a culvert, pipe, or channel.

diversion

A channel with or without a supporting ridge on the lower side, constructed across a slope to intercept surface runoff.

DTM - DEM

A Digital Terrain Model / Digital Elevation Model is a digital representation of the earth's surface.

drainage

The interception and removal of groundwater or surface water by artificial or natural means.

drainage area

The area drained by a channel or subsurface drain.

DXF file

Data Exchange Format. DXF is an ASCII Format and can be opened in every text editor.

---

elevation

The altitude of a given point relative to a given datum.

embankment

A bank of earth, rock, or other material constructed above the natural ground surface.

erodibility

The susceptibility of soil material to become detached and transported by running water or wind.

erosion

The detachment and movement of soil or rock fragments by water, wind, ice and gravity.

excavation

The act of extracting material from the earth.

---

fill

The part of the ground surface which, when graded, is higher than the original ground.

filter strip

A vegetated buffer zone for removing sediments and pollutants before runoff reaches ponds, waterways, or other drainage facilities.

fine grade

Accurate preparation of the subbases and surfacing that precedes installation of the final surfacing material.

finished grade

The completed level of hard and soft surfaces such as lawns, pathways, and roads brought to grade as designed.

foundation

The portion of a structure (usually below ground level) that distributes pressure onto the soil or to artificial supports.

free water

Soil water that moves by gravity, in contrast to capillary and hydroscopic water.

French drain

A trench filled with coarse aggregate (with or without a pipe) for intercepting and conveying groundwater.

fascine

A fascine is a bundles of branches, tied together and used for slope stabilization.

---

gabion

A compartmented rectangular container, made of steel wire mesh, and filled with stone. Gabions are used for erosion control and retaining walls.

geodetic

A basic relationship with the Earth that takes into account the curvature of the Earth's sea level surface. For example, a geodetic distance is a distance or angle in which the Earth's curvature is taken into account, versus a distance or angle measured on a flat paper map.

geosynthetics

Degradable and nondegradable products used for a variety of purposes, including soil and slope stabilization, erosion and sediment control, soil reinforcement, and subsurface drainage.

geotextiles

Woven and nonwoven permeable fabrics and grids used for soil-related construction projects.

grade

The slope of a plot of land. Grading is the mechanical process of moving earth and thereby changing the degree of rise or descent of the land in order to establish good drainage and otherwise suit the intent of a landscape design.

gradient

The degree of inclination of a surface, road, or pipe, usually expressed as a percentage.

grading

The modification of the ground surface by cut and/or fill. Fine or finish grading is light or thin grading to finish a prepared ground surface.

gravel

Small particle size rock, typically 2 to 75 mm in

diameter. Used in base and subbase aggregate, crushed or uncrushed, often mixed with sand.

groundwater

Free subsurface water, the top of which is the water table.

GPS

Global Positioning System

geo-reference

A point assigned with accurate real-world co-ordinates in a map projection of the geometric representation of an object.

grading plan

A document – often a contour plan – that provides information for the grading process.

ha-ha

A ha-ha creates a barrier for sheep, cattle and deer, while allowing an unbroken view of the landscape.

hardscape

The hard elements added to a natural landscape, such as paving stones, gravel, walkways, irrigation systems, roads, retaining walls, sculpture, street amenities, fountains, and other mechanical features.

headwall

A vertical wall at the end of a culvert to support the pipe and prevent earth from spilling into the channel.

hydrologic condition

A term describing the vegetative cover, residue, and surface roughness of a soil as they affect potential runoff.

hedge layer

Seedlings in rows covered by soil used in soil stabilization.

imperviousness

The property of a material through which water will not flow under ordinary hydrostatic pressure.

infiltration

The downward entry of water into the surface

of a soil or other material, as contrasted with percolation, which is the movement of water through soil layers or material.

infiltration basin

An open surface storage area with no outlet except an emergency spillway, which permits rain-water runoff to infiltrate into the soil.

inlet

An opening that conveys surface water, for example, to a drain.

intercepting ditch

An open drain that prevents surface water from flowing down a slope by conducting it around the slope.

interpolation

The process of determining the location of elevations from the plotted locations of known elevations.

invert

The lowest point of the internal cross section of a pipe or a channel.

live fascines

Long, bound, sausage-like bundles of live cut branches that are placed in shallow trenches, partly covered with soil, and staked in place to prevent erosion and soil slippage.

LandXML

LandXML is an open source exchange format used in civil engineering and GIS.

live stake

A cutting from a living branch that is tamped or inserted into the earth and that will eventually root and sprout leaves.

living brush mattress

Branches several meters long fixed by poles and wire and used for soil protection.

manhole

A structure, covered with a lid, that allows access to a space below ground level.

moisture content

The percentage, by weight, of water contained

in soil or other material, usually based on dry weight.

natural grade

The undisturbed natural surface of the ground.

outlet

Point of water exit from a stream, river, lake, tidewater, water feature or artificial drain.

parent material

Unconsolidated, slightly weathered rocky mass from which soil develops.

peak discharge

The maximum instantaneous flow rate resulting from a given storm condition at a specific location

percolation

The movement of soil water toward the water table.

pervious

The property of a material that permits movement of water through it under ordinary hydrostatic pressure.

porous

Having many small openings through which liquids may pass.

porous pavement

A pavement constructed from a material that permits the percolation of storm water to the subgrade.

planting plan

A document, often a drawing superimposed upon a grading plan, showing the location, size and species of new plants in a proposed planting design.

rainfall intensity (i)

The rate at which rain falls, measured in millimeters per hour (mm/h)

ramp

An inclined plane connecting two different levels.

retaining wall

A wall built to structurally support an embankment of earth.

right of way

A strip of land, the use of which is granted for transportation such as rail or highway; or a path, road, or accessway where use for transportation is permitted.

riprap

Stones or other material placed on a slope to prevent erosion by water.

rough grade

The stage of the grading operation in which the desired landform is approximately attained.

runoff

Precipitation that flows away from the area onto which it falls.

reinforced earth

The installation of wire fabric and or geotextiles in soil embankments in order to stabilize the steep slope face.

rock-filled woven wire mat, gabion mat

Prefabricated wire mesh boxes filled with stones.

rhombic wattling

Geotextile with a honeycomb form.

sediment

Solid material, both mineral and organic, in suspension, being transported or having been moved from its original site by air, water, gravity or ice.

seepage ditch

Sloped ditches filled with material that is pervious to water (rubble drain).

shear stress

The force per unit area exerted in parallel or tangential to the face of the material.

shoulder

The portion of roadway between the edge of the hardened wearing course and the ditch or embankment.

slope protection mats

Temporary protection of slopes by mats, made from materials such as hemp, reed, coconut fibers, and so forth.

softscape

The natural elements with which landscape architects work, such as plant materials and the soil itself.

slide

The movement of soil on a slope resulting in a reduced angle of repose, usually occurring as the result of rainfall, high water or thaw.

slope

The face of an embankment or cut section. Any ground with a surface that makes an angle with the level horizon.

sod rolls

Precultivated lawn grass in rolls.

soil bioengineering

Use of live, woody, vegetative cuttings to repair slope failures and increase slope stability.

spot elevation

A three-dimensional point with a specific location and elevation used to describe terrain, paving or other fixed elevations.

storm sewer

A conduit, typically underground, used to convey rainwater.

structure

Anything constructed that requires a permanent location on the ground or is attached to something that has a permanent location on the ground.

subgrade

The native soil material, which is graded and compacted to provide the foundation for a surfacing material, such as under roads, paths, lawns and other landscape works.

subsoil

The soil below plow depth, brown or reddish in color.

subsurface drainage

The use of plastic, clay or concrete pipes for a controlled waterflow away from a structure.

survey marker / survey monument

A boundary stone or other permanent marker locating a property line, corner or important survey point.

swale

A constructed or natural grassed or vegetated concave landform, used to cleanse, convey and infiltrate rainwater runoff.

---

tangent

A straight road segment connecting two curves.

terrace

An essentially level and defined area.

trench drain

A linear structure that collects runoff from a paved area.

TIN

Triangulated Irregular Network.

terracing

The construction of terraced landforms.

tumulus

An ancient cairn or burial mound.

---

vegetated structures

A retaining wall system in which living plants or cuttings have been integrated into the structure.

vegetated cuttings

Live, cut stems and branches of plants that will root when planted or inserted into the ground.

---

water table

The level below which the ground is saturated with water.

watershed

The area of land from which all water drains to a single specified point.

wet sowing

Hydroseeding. Seeds as well as straw and glue are sprayed onto the soil.

wattle fence

Living twigs are woven around stakes and used to stabilize the soil.

Andrews, John / Bostwick, Todd (2000): *Desert Farmers at the River's Edge. The Hohokam and Pueblo Grande.* Pueblo Grande Museum and Archaeological Park, Phoenix, Arizona.

Baukader Schweiz, ed. (2006): *Taschenbuch für Bauführer und Poliere.* Baukader Schweiz, Olten.

Beier, Harm-Eckart / Niesel, Alfred / Pätzold, Heiner (2003): *Lehr-Taschenbuch für den Garten-, Landschafts- und Sportplatzbau.* Ulmer, Stuttgart.

Bishop, Ian / Lange, Eckart (2005): *Visualization in Landscape and Environmental Planning.* Taylor & Francis, London.

Buhmann, Erich / Paar, Philip / Bishop, Ian / Lange, Eckart (2005): *Trends in Real-Time Landscape Visualization and Participation.* Proceedings at Anhalt University of Applied Sciences. Wichmann, Heidelberg.

Buhmann, Erich / Ervin, Stephen (2003): *Trends in Landscape Modeling.* Proceedings at Anhalt University of Applied Sciences. Wichmann, Heidelberg.

Bürgi, Andreas (2007): *Relief der Urschweiz.* Neue Zürcher Zeitung, Zurich.

Carter, George / Goode, Patrick / Kedrun, Laurie (1982): *Humphry Repton Landscape Gardener 1752–1818.* Sainsbury Centre for Visual Arts Publication, University of East Anglia, Norwich.

Coors, Volker / Zipf, Alexander (2005): *3D-Geoinformationssysteme.* Wichmann, Heidelberg.

Eidenbenz, Mathias (2001): *"Technologie aus der Froschperspektive",* in: tec21, 15/2001, Zurich, pp. 7–12.

Ervin, Stephen / Hasbrouck, Hope (2001): *Landscape Modeling. Digital Techniques for Landscape Visualization.* McGraw-Hill, New York.

FaBo, Fachstelle Bodenschutz, Canton Zurich, ed. (2003): *Rekultivierung von Böden. Erläuterungen zu den Richtlinien für Bodenrekultivierungen.* ‹www.fabo.zh.ch›

FGSV Forschungsgesellschaft für Strassen- und Verkehrswesen (2003): *Merkblatt über Stützkonstruktionen aus Betonelementen, Blockschichtungen und Gabionen.*

FLL Forschungsgesellschaft Landschaftsentwicklung und Landschaftsbau e.V. (1998): *Empfehlungen zur Begrünung von Problemflächen.* Bonn.

Florineth, Florin (2004): *Pflanzen statt Beton. Handbuch zur Ingenieurbiologie und Vegetationstechnik.* Patzer, Berlin.

Grzimek, Günther (1993): *"Olympische Park-Ideen",* in: *Garten + Landschaft – Zeitschrift für Landschaftsarchitektur.* Issue 9/1993. Callwey, Munich, pp. 31–35.

Grzimek, Günther (1984): *"Parks und Gärten. Mit Grün gegen die Versteinerung",* in: *Naturraum Menschenlandschaft.* Peter K. Köhler, ed.,

Meyster, Munich, pp. 59–73.

Grzimek, Günther (1973): *Gedanken zur Stadt- und Landschaftsarchitektur seit Friedrich Ludwig v. Sckell.* Series by the Bavarian Academy of Fine Arts, no. 11. Callwey, Munich.

Grzimek, Günther (1972): "Spiel und Sport im Olympiapark München", in: *Spiel und Sport in der Stadtlandschaft.* Series by the Deutschen Gesellschaft für Gartenkunst und Landschaftspflege, vol. 9. Callwey, Munich, pp. 10–49.

Gugerli, David, ed. (1999): *Vermessene Landschaften. Kulturgeschichte und technische Praxis im 19. und 20. Jahrhundert.* Chronos, Zurich.

Harley, J.B. / Woodward, D., eds. (1987): *History of Cartography, Volume I, Cartography in the Prehistoric, Ancient and Medieval Europe and the Mediterranean.* University of Chicago Press, Chicago.

Henz, L. (1856): *Praktische Anleitungen zum Erdbau.* Ernst & Korn. Berlin.

Henz, Thomas (1984): *Gestaltung Städtischer Freiräume.* Patzer, Berlin.

Imhof, Eduard (1965): *Kartographische Geländedarstellung.* Walter De Gruyter & Co., Berlin.

Imhof, Eduard (1968): *Gelände und Karte.* Eugen Rentsch, Zurich.

Jencks, Charles (2005): *Im Kosmos des Charles Jencks.* ZDF, DVD series, Neue Gartenkunst, Mainz.

Kassler, Elizabeth (1964): *Modern Gardens and the Landscape.* The Museum of Modern Art, New York.

Knaupe, Werner (1975): *Erdbau.* Bertelsmann, Düsseldorf.

Kohlschmidt, Siegfried (1999): "Der Fürst und sein Geheimsekretär. Spurensuche im Briefwechsel Fürst Pückler und Wilhelm Heinrich Masser", in: *Pückler Pyramiden Panorama. Neue Beiträge zur Pücklerforschung.* Foundation for the Fürst-

Pückler Museum – Branitz Park and Schloss, publication No. 4. Cottbus, pp. 169–195.

Landphair, Harlow / Klatt, Fred (1979): *Landscape Architecture Construction.* Elsevier, New York.

Lauer, Udo (1996): *Fürst Pücklers Traumpark. Schloss Branitz.* Ullstein, Berlin.

Loidl, Hans (1990): *Objektplanung. Materialien zu einer Morphologie des Freiraumentwurfs.* Transcript from the seminar "Objektplanung", TU Berlin, p. 34.

Lynch, Kevin (1962): *Site Planning.* M.I.T. Press, Cambridge, Massachusetts.

Mach, Rüdiger / Petschek, Peter (2006): *Visualisierung digitaler Gelände- und Landschaftsdaten.* Springer, Berlin, Heidelberg.

Mader, Günther (1999): *Gartenkunst des 20. Jahrhunderts. Garten und Landschaftsarchitektur in Deutschland.* DVA, Stuttgart, pp. 158–163.

Margolis, Liat / Robinson, Alexander (2007): *Living Systems.* Birkhäuser, Basel, Boston, Berlin.

Miller, C.L. / Laflamme, R.A. (1958): "The Digital Terrain Model – Theory & Application", in: *Photogrammetric Engineering*, Vol. XXIV, No. 3, June 1958. The American Society of Photogrammetry.

Neumann, Siegfried (1999): "Die Begräbnisstätten im Branitzer Park", in: *Pückler Pyramiden Panorama. Neue Beiträge zur Pücklerforschung.* Foundation for the Fürst-Pückler Museum – Branitz Park and Schloss, publication no. 4. Cottbus, pp. 7–18.

Petschek, Peter / Lange, Eckart (2003): *Open space Planning—The Use of New Media and 3D Visualization in the Development Case Study Site Zurich-Leutschenbach (CTI research project, project summary). Available at ‹ilf.hsr.ch/fileadmin/user_upload/ilf.hsr.ch/4_Projekte/Projektbericht.pdf›.*

Pückler-Muskau, Hermann Fürst von (1988): *Andeutungen über Landschaftsgärtnerei ver-*

bunden mit der Beschreibung ihrer praktischen Anwendung in Muskau. Günther J. Vaupel ed., Insel, Frankfurt a. M.

Richter, Dietrich / Heindel, Manfred (2004): Straßen- und Tiefbau. Teubner, Wiesbaden.
Rüegger, Rudolf / Hufenus, Rudolf (2003): *Bauen mit Geokunststoffen.* SVG Schweizerischer Verband für Geokunststoffe, St. Gallen.

Schäfer, Anne (1999): "Bleyers Arbeiten im Branitzer Park", in: *Pückler Pyramiden Panorama. Neue Beiträge zur Pücklerforschung.* Foundation for the Fürst-Pückler Museum – Branitz Park and Schloss, publication no. 4. Cottbus, pp. 129–142.
Schatz, Rudolf / Lehr, Richard (1970): *Feldmessen im Garten- und Landschaftsbau.* Paul Parey, Berlin.
Schilling, Alexander (2007): *Modellbau.* Birkhäuser, Basel, Boston, Berlin.
Schlüter, Uwe (1996): *Pflanze als Baustoff.* Patzer, Berlin, Hanover.
Schulz, Georg (1995): *Lexikon zur Bestimmung der Geländeform in Karten.* Berliner geographische Studien, vol. 28, Berlin.
Sckell, Friedrich Ludwig von (1825): *Beiträge zur bildenden Gartenkunst für angehende Gartenkünstler und Gartenliebhaber.* Werner'sche Verlagsgesellschaft, Worms. New edition 1982.
Sckell, Friedrich Ludwig von (1818): *Beiträge zur bildenden Gartenkunst für angehende Gartenkünstler und Gartenliebhaber.* Joseph Lindauer, Munich.
Strom, Steven / Nathan, Kurt (1998): *Site Engineering for Landscape Architects.* Wiley, New York.

Tietze, Christian (1999): "Pyramiden in Brandenburg", in: *Pückler Pyramiden Panorama. Neue Beiträge zur Pücklerforschung.* Foundation for the Fürst-Pückler Museum – Branitz Park and Schloss, publication no. 4. Cottbus, pp. 19–40.

Treib, Marc / Herman, Ron (1980): *A Guide to the Gardens of Kyoto.* Shufunotomo Company, Tokyo.

Untermann, Richard (1973): *Grade Easy.* Landscape Architecture Foundation, Washington D.C.

Weilacher, Udo (2001): *Visionary Gardens: The Modern Landscape of Ernst Cramer.* Birkhäuser, Basel, Boston, Berlin.
Westort, Caroline (2001): *Digital Earth Moving. First International Symposium, DEM 2001, Manno, Switzerland, September 2001, Proceedings.* Springer, Heidelberg.
Wilhelmy, Herbert (1972): *Kartographie in Stichworten. II Karteninhalt und Kartenwerke.* Ferdinand Hirt, Kiel.

Zeh, Helgard (2007): *Ingenieurbiologie. Handbuch der Bautypen.* VDF Swiss Federal Institute of Technology (ETH), Zurich.

Picture Credits / Table Credits

All pictures originate with the author, with the exception of those listed below:

Albanese & Lutzke, Albanese Paul: 9.14

Archiv für Schweizer Landschaftsarchitektur (SLA), Rapperswil, Ernst Cramer Collection: 3.29, 3.30, 3.31, 3.32, 3.33, 3.34, 3.35

asp Landschaftsarchitekten / Neuenschwander: 2.4 Irchelpark, University of Zurich

Bolliger Peter, Prof: 4.2, 4.3

Bünzli D., Ingenieurbüro Bünzli AG: 9.11

Burkart Hans-Peter: 4.1, 5.55, 5.56, 5.57, 5.58, 5.59, 5.60

Cavigelli GaLaBau: 6.15, 6.18

C-Technik Software GmbH, Pook Michael: 7.23

Deponie Tüfentobel, St. Gallen: 7.25

Fluss Michael: 2.5, 6.4, 6.5, 6.6, 6.7, 6.8, 6.12, 6.14, 6.16, 6.17, 6.20

Foundation for the Fürst-Pückler Museum – Branitz Park and Schloss: 3.23, 3.24, 3.25

Geitz + Partner, Freie Garten- und Landschaftsarchitekten, Stuttgart: 8.10, 8.11, 8.12, 8.24

Glacier Garden, Lucerne: 7.22

Harradine Golf: 3.9, 10.1, 10.2, 10.3, 10.4

Henz L.: 3.21, 3.22

Ian White Associates, Landscape Architects & Planners, Stirling, UK: 3.52, 3.53, 3.54, 3.55, 3.56, 3.57

ilu AG Ingenieure, Landschaftsarchitekten, Umweltfachleute, Uster: 10.19 to 10.37

Inauen Bruno, Inauen-Koch und KIBAG Uster/Zürich: 8.18, 8.19, 8.20

Kandzia Christian, South West German Architecture and Engineering Archive (Südwestdeutsches Archiv für Architektur und Ingenieurbau), University of Karlsruhe, Günter Behnisch & Partner collection: 3.39, 3.45, 3.46, 3.47

Leica Geosystems, Heerbrugg: 7.5, 7.7, 9.2, 9.47, 9.48

Lukas Domeisen AG: 5.82

Maurer Yves, HSR: 1.3, 4.25, 9.35 to 9.38

NASA-Johnson Space Center: 10.12, image courtesy of Earth Sciences and Image Analysis Laboratory, ISS011-E-10319, http://eol.jsc.nasa.gov

Orient Irrigation Services, Heiko Heinig: 8.6, 10.5, 10.6, 10.7, 10.8, 10.9, 10.10, 10.11, 10.13, 10.14, 10.15, 10.16 , 10.17, 10.18

Peter Walker and Partners (PWP): 1.2

Pöyry Infra AG, Laager Peter: 8.14, 8.15

Rehau AG: 6.13

RIBA Library Drawings Collection: 9.1

RSI GmbH: 7.28

Rutishauser Landschaftsarchitekten: 5.1

Schildwächter Ingenieure: 7.32

South West German Architecture and Engineering Archive (Südwestdeutsches Archiv für Architektur und Ingenieurbau), University of Karlsruhe, Günter Behnisch & Partner collection: 3.40, 3.41, 3.42, 3.43 , 3.44

Städtische Sammlung Cottbus, Stadtarchiv: 3.20

Swiss Federal Institute of Technology (ETH Zurich) Library, Old Prints Collection: 3.21, 3.22, 9.5

Swiss Federal Office of Topography (swisstopo): 3.4 Dufour map extract, reproduced with permission from swisstopo. 3.8 Türlersee (BA071439), reproduced with permission from swisstopo.

SYTEC, Sacchetti Toni: 8.21, 8.22, 8.23, 8.28, 8.29

Toller Unternehmungen AG. Garten, Strassen- und Tiefbau, Eschenbach: 9.18 to 9.34

University of Heidelberg Library: 3.2, 3.3

Utrecht University Library, "De Boven-Merwede" by Nicolaas Cruquius, 1730: 3.6, 3.7

UMS GmbH, Environmental Monitoring Systems: 8.3

Westrag AG, M. Bamert: 9.44, 9.45, 9.46

Zentralbibliothek Zurich: 3.1 Federation map by Konrad Türst, 1495/1497.

ZÜND Systemtechnik AG: 7.24

Table 1 to 4 originate with the author.